REAL-WORLD MATHEMATICS THROUGH SCIENCE

IN THE WIND

Christine V. Johnson

Nancy Cook, Project Director

Developed by Washington MESA

Funded by the Discuren Foundation

Dale Seymour Publications®

MESA wishes to express its appreciation to these people for their advice and assistance, without which this module could not have been completed:

Nancy Cook, Project Director
Washington MESA
University of Washington
Seattle, Washington

Christine V. Johnson
Washington MESA
University of Washington
Seattle, Washington

Bob Kelley-Wickemeyer
The Boeing Company
Seattle, Washington

Washington MESA middle school mathematics and science teachers in Seattle, Spokane, Tacoma, Toppenish, and Yakima, Washington

Project Editor: Joan Gideon
Production/Manufacturing: Joe Conte
Design Manager: Jeff Kelly
Text Design: Michelle Taverniti
Text Illustration: Carl Yoshihara and Rachel Gage
Cover Design: Dennis Teutschel
Cover Photograph: David W. Hamilton, Image Bank West
Photograph on page 115 is from the collection of the Henry Ford Museum
    and Greenfield Village.

This book is published by Dale Seymour Publications®, an imprint of Addison Wesley Longman, Inc.

Many of the designations used by manufacturers and sellers to distinguish their products are claimed as trademarks. Where those designations appear in this book and Addison Wesley Longman was aware of a trademark claim, the designations have been printed with initial capital letters.

Funded by the Discuren Foundation. This material in part is based on work supported by Grant No. MDR-8751287 from the National Science Foundation; Instructional Materials Development; Arlington, VA 22230. The material was designed and developed by Washington MESA (Mathematics, Engineering, Science Achievement); University of Washington; 353 Loew Hall Box 352181; Seattle, WA 98195-2181. Any opinions, findings, conclusions, or recommendations expressed in this publication are those of Washington MESA and do not necessarily reflect the views of the National Science Foundation.

ISBN 0-201-49606-2
DS 22736
2 3 4 5 6 7 8 9 10—ML–00-99 98 97

IN THE WIND

CONTENTS

Introduction   vi
Conceptual Overview   viii
Activity Overview   ix
Materials List   xi
Resources List   xiv

Activity 1. Navigation and Aviation   1
Technology Link: The Voyage of *Voyager*   12
Career Link: Airline Pilots   13
Student Sheet 1.1   Navigation   14
Student Sheet 1.2   Flight Paths   15
Student Sheet 1.3   A 1,000-Mile Journey   17
Transparency Master 1.4   Navigation and Aviation   19

Activity 2. Drifting Apart   20
History Link: Amelia Earhart   30
Interest Link: What if You Are Off Course?   31
Student Sheet 2.1   Plane Tracks   33
Student Sheet 2.2   Catch My Drift?   36
Student Sheet 2.3   Degrees of Drift   37
Transparency Master 2.4   Drifting Apart   40

Activity 3. Blowing in the Wind   42
Interest Link: Wind   54
Career Link: Meteorologists   55
Student Sheet 3.1   Windy Conditions   56
Student Sheet 3.2   Wind Parallelograms   57
Student Sheet 3.3   Wind Shifts   59
Student Sheet 3.4   Wind Speeds   62

Activity 4. When the Wind Blows   64

Technology Link: Wind Shear   72
Interest Link: Weather Conditions   73
Student Sheet 4.1   Where the Wind Blows   75
Student Sheet 4.2   Parallelogram Plots   76
Student Sheet 4.3   Vector Ventures   78
Student Sheet 4.4   Sum Vectors   79
Student Sheet 4.5   May the Force Be with You   80
Student Sheet 4.6   Plane Techniques   82

Activity 5. Back on Track   84

Writing Link: Winds Aloft   95
Interest Link: Learning to Fly   97
Student Sheet 5.1   True Heading   98
Student Sheet 5.2   Wind Correction   100
Student Sheet 5.3   Diagonals and Differences   102
Student Sheet 5.4   Track and True   104
Student Sheet 5.5   As the Wind Blows   105
Transparency Master 5.6   Back on Track   107

Family Activity: Wind Tunnel   108

Technology Link: Wind Tunnels   114
Career Link: Aeronautical Engineer   116
Family Activity Sheet 1   What Makes an Airplane Fly?   118
Family Activity Sheet 2   Four Forces in Flight and Air Flow   120
Family Activity Sheet 3   Making a Wind Tunnel   121
Family Activity Sheet 4   Wind Tunnel Tests   123
Completed Student Sheets   125
Grid Paper   141

INTRODUCTION

In the Wind is one of the middle-grades instructional modules created and field-tested by the Washington MESA (Mathematics, Engineering, Science Achievement) project. Washington MESA operates on the premise that effective classroom materials should facilitate connections between classroom and real-world mathematics and science. Staff members and teachers work with scientists, mathematicians, and engineers to outline each module. Pilot modules are tested in middle school classrooms, then revised using feedback from the teachers.

The modules weave important mathematics themes with relevant, exciting science topics. The activities are based on current reform philosophies recommended by the National Council of Teachers of Mathematics' *Curriculum and Evaluation Standards for School Mathematics* and the American Association for the Advancement of Science's *Project 2061*. Students will

◆ learn by doing. Students simulate a flight situation to discover the actual path an airplane follows while being continuously pushed off course by the wind.

◆ employ a variety of reasoning processes by using several mathematics approaches to solve similar problems.

◆ learn to express technical concepts as they write and discuss answers to open-ended questions. The questions are designed to provoke further thought about how science and mathematics connect to the everyday world.

◆ learn the appropriate use of calculators by solving real problems. Students are taught how to conceptualize and set up problems that they can then solve using calculators.

◆ make connections between mathematics and science as well as connections within mathematics and science. Writing Link, History Link, Career Link, Technology Link, and Interest Link activities are included to expand the connections to other subject areas.

◆ explore careers by simulating professional roles in the activities. Students also study jobs that use mathematics and science in the Career Link features.

In the Wind directs middle school students toward active involvement in learning. Students emulate real-world work environments by collaborating in small groups and striving for group consensus. They work with concrete materials and evaluate open-ended problems. This combined approach helps students make the transition from concrete to abstract thinking, a transition that is crucial to the intellectual development of students at this age. Assessment is integrated into *In the Wind* activities. Assessment goals and instruction goals are identical.

Family encouragement can help students to succeed educationally, so a special activity involves families in hands-on, collaborative work. As they work with parents and family members, students learn to build a simple wind tunnel to test the aerodynamics and flight patterns of various objects.

Each activity begins with an Overview page summarizing what students will be doing and how the teacher needs to prepare. This is followed by background information for the teacher's use and a Presenting the Activity section, which describes the activity in detail and suggests discussion and assessment questions. This is followed by Student Sheets and Transparency Masters in blackline master form (completed Student Sheets are provided on pages 125–140). Career Link, History Link, Writing Link, Technology Link, and Interest Link features are found throughout the book.

CONCEPTUAL OVERVIEW

In the Wind addresses the following mathematics topics, science topics, and NCTM standards.

NCTM Curriculum Standards

Problem Solving
  Open-Ended
  Multiple Strategies
Communication
  Verbal and Written
Reasoning
  Logical and Spatial
  Predictions and Evaluations
Mathematical Connections
  Among Topics
  To Real-World Contexts

NCTM Teaching Standards

Worthwhile Tasks
  Real-World Contexts
Teacher's Role
  Listening and Observing
  Orchestrating Discourse
Enhancement Tools
  Calculators
  Concrete Materials
Learning Environment
  Collaborative Work

NCTM Evaluation Standards

Alignment
  Integral to Instruction
Multiple Sources
  Oral and Written
  Individual and Group
Multiple Methods
  Instructional Planning
  Grading
Mathematical Power
  Communicating
  Reasoning
  Integrating
  Generalizing

Mathematics Content

Number Relationships
  Ratios
  Integers
  Decimals
Computation and Estimation
  Time Calculations
  Mental Arithmetic
  Calculators
  Estimation
  Rounding
Patterns and Functions
  Pattern Investigations
  Representing Situations
    with Verbal Rules
    and Equations
  Analyzing Tables
Measurement
  Angle Measures
  Distances
  Metric and Standard
  Rates

Mathematics Content

Geometry
  Angles
  Scale Drawings
  Parallel Lines
  Equilateral Triangles
  Parallelogram Properties
  Vector Properties
Statistics
  Data Collection
  Inferences

Science Topics

Navigation
  Orientation
  Compass Headings
  Effects of Wind

Science Topics

Map Reading
  State Maps
  Map Scales
Wind Tunnel
  Design Process
  Testing Procedures
Physics
  Speed, Distance, Time
  Vector Quantities
  Principles of Flight
  Bernoulli's Principle
Scientific Process
  Predicting
  Hypothesizing
  Analyzing
  Concluding
Weather Forecasts
  Wind Condition
  Air Pressure

ACTIVITY OVERVIEW

Overview

Many middle school students are familiar with the MESA module *In the Air*. As a result, they may know how to use a state map to chart an aeronautical course using navigation techniques. However, they are probably unfamiliar with how wind influences the path of an airplane, the methods pilots use to counteract this force, and the career of an aeronautical engineer.

Activities in *In the Wind* explore the mathematics and methods pilots use to navigate in windy conditions. They emphasize the mathematical connections for determining the correct headings to fly on a cross-country journey in a Cessna 172 when forecast winds are present.

If possible, invite a pilot or aeronautical engineer to visit the class. They will be able to answer questions and present specific instances of how wind affects flight and aircraft design.

Activity 1: Navigation and Aviation

Students review charting an aeronautical course. They use laminated state maps to chart course lines between airports. Using circular protractors, they determine directions then calculate distances and flight times. They discover mathematical relationships between parallel course lines and in the degree measures for initial and return flights. Working in pairs, students prepare a detailed flight plan for a 1,000-mile journey in a Cessna 172, incorporating a head wind and a tail wind. Finally, they examine an aeronautical sectional chart to locate familiar landmarks and to interpret symbols.

Activity 2: Drifting Apart

Students discover the path an airplane follows when continuously pushed off course by wind. They recognize how slight to moderate changes in a compass heading might effect their location. Using scale drawings on grid paper, students simulate aeronautical experiences as they extend course lines to examine the relationship between the distance traveled on an incorrect heading and the number of miles a pilot is off course. The concept of *drift angle* is introduced.

Activity 3: Blowing in the Wind

Students continue to investigate the path an airplane follows as it is continuously pushed off course by wind. Working in pairs, they use tractor-feed strips from used computer paper or Polystrips™ to build models of wind parallelograms, which are used to determine the actual flight path. Students investigate the effect wind has on the ground track and ground speed of an airplane. Through this, they are introduced to the concept of *vector*.

Activity 4: When the Wind Blows

Forecast information provides the direction from which the wind is blowing. Students use such data to determine the direction toward which the wind is blowing an airplane. After students are introduced to vectors, they use them to determine the effect wind has on a planned flight course, relating the situations to their previous work with wind parallelograms. Vectors are then applied to establish an airplane's ground track and ground speed.

Activity 5: Back on Track

Students revisit several previous flight situations to determine the true heading a pilot must follow to compensate for the prevailing winds. They explore a parallelogram method using tractor-feed strips or Polystrips™ before investigating a technique using vectors to identify the true heading and to calculate the adjusted ground speed. Students apply wind conditions to each leg of their original 1,000-mile journeys and complete detailed flight plans. The total times for their journeys are reassessed and compared to their original flight expectations from Activity 1, in which wind was not taken into account.

Family Activity: Wind Tunnel

Students are introduced to the forces involved in the theory of flight—lift, drag, weight, and thrust. With their families, they conduct several experiments that illustrate Bernoulli's principle, the scientific basis behind aircraft design. Families build simple wind tunnels in which to test the aerodynamics of various objects. Students begin to understand career aspects of aeronautical engineers.

MATERIALS LIST

Activity	Materials Required
Navigation and Aviation	*For each student:* ◆ Student Sheets 1.1–1.3 ◆ Circular protractor *For each pair of students:* ◆ Laminated state map ◆ Ruler ◆ Overhead transparency pens ◆ Calculator ◆ Spray bottle ◆ Rag or sponge ◆ Yardstick ◆ Aeronautical sectional chart *For the teacher:* ◆ Aeronautical chart for display ◆ Transparencies of Student Sheets 1.1–1.3 (optional) ◆ Transparency Master 1.4 ◆ Blank transparency
Drifting Apart	*For each student:* ◆ Student Sheets 2.1–2.3 ◆ Ruler ◆ Circular protractor ◆ Copy of History Link "Amelia Earhart" (page 30) ◆ Copy of Interest Link "What if You Are Off Course?" (page 31) *For each pair of students:* ◆ Calculator ◆ Grid paper ◆ Marks-A-Lot® pen *For the teacher:* ◆ Transparencies of Student Sheets 2.1–2.3 (optional) ◆ Transparency Master 2.4

Blowing in the Wind

For each student:
◆ Completed Student Sheet 2.1 (for reference)
◆ Student Sheets 3.1–3.4
◆ Circular protractor
◆ Ruler

For each pair of students:
◆ Calculator
◆ Grid paper
◆ Tractor-feed strips from used computer paper or Polystrips™
◆ 8 brads

For the teacher:
◆ Transparencies of Student Sheets 3.1–3.4 (optional)
◆ Transparency of grid paper

When the Wind Blows

For each student:
◆ Student Sheets 4.1–4.6
◆ Circular protractor
◆ Ruler

For each pair of students:
◆ Calculator
◆ Tractor-feed strips from used computer paper or Polystrips™
◆ 8 brads
◆ Laminated state map
◆ Rag or sponge
◆ Overhead transparency pen
◆ Spray bottle
◆ Yardstick
◆ Grid paper

For the teacher:
◆ Transparencies of Student Sheets 4.1–4.6 (optional)

Back on Track

For each student:
◆ Student Sheets 5.1–5.5
◆ Completed Student Sheets 1.3, 3.3, 4.4, and 4.6
◆ Ruler
◆ Circular protractor
◆ Grid paper
◆ Writing Link: Winds Aloft

For each pair of students:
◆ Tractor-feed strips from used computer paper or Polystrips™
◆ 8 brads
◆ Highlighter pen
◆ Calculator
◆ Construction compass

For the teacher:
◆ Transparencies of Student Sheets 5.1–5.5 (optional)
◆ Transparency Master 5.6

Wind Tunnel

For each family group:
◆ Family Activity Sheets 1–4
◆ Notebook paper
◆ Scissors
◆ Paper clips
◆ 2 large, identical cardboard boxes
◆ Electric fan
◆ 4–8 sets of identical box inserts used to separate glass bottles
◆ 1 small utility hook
◆ Transparency
◆ Masking tape
◆ Lightweight string
◆ Tape measure or ruler
◆ Knife
◆ Objects for flight testing (see Family Activity Sheet 3)

For the teacher:
◆ Transparency of Family Activity Sheet 2

RESOURCES LIST

This list of resources was compiled by teachers, scientists, and professionals who participated in developing *In the Wind*. It is intended for teachers who would like to pursue the topic further with their classes, for small groups of students who are particularly interested in the topic, for individual students who desire further investigations, or for the teacher's own professional development.

1. Aviator Store
   7201 Perimeter Road S., Boeing Field
   Seattle, WA 98108
   (206) 763-0666

2. Wings Aloft
   Aircraft Flying School
   8467 Perimeter Road S., Boeing Field
   Seattle, WA 98108
   (206) 763-2113

3. National Oceanic and Atmospheric Administration (NOAA)
   Distribution Division
   66501 Lafayette Avenue
   Riverdale, MD 20840
   (301) 436-6990

4. C-Thru Ruler Company
   6 Britton Drive
   Bloomfield, CT 06002
   (203) 243-0303

5. Polystrips™
   Cuisenaire Company of America
   P.O. Box 5026
   White Plains, NY 10602-5026
   (800) 237-0338

6. King of the Road Map Service, Inc.
   P.O. Box 55758
   Seattle, WA 98155
   (800) 223-8852

7. Federal Aviation Administration
   Northwest Aviation Education Officer
   1601 Lind Avenue, SW
   Renton, WA 98055-4056

8. American Institute of Aeronautics and Astronautics
   Student Programs Department
   The Aerospace Center
   370 L'Enfant Promenade, SW
   Washington, D.C. 20024-2518

9. Garder, Robert. *The Complete Private Pilot*. Renton, Wash.: Aviation Supplies and Academics, Inc., 1992.

10. *Flight Training Handbook*. Washington, D.C.: Federal Aviation Administration, 1980.

11. Maloney, Elbert S. *Dutton's Navigation and Piloting*. Annapolis, Md.: Naval Institute Press, 1978.

12. Dye, Aimee. *Aviation Curriculum Guide for Middle School Level*. Washington D.C.: Federal Aviation Administration, 1984.

13. *Aviation Science Activities for Elementary Grades*. Washington, D.C.: Federal Aviation Administration, 1983.

14. Ludington, Charles. *Smoke Streams*. New York: Coward-McCann, 1943.

15. Mander, Jerry, George Dippel, and Howard Gossage. *The Great International Paper Airplane Book*. New York: Simon and Schuster, 1967.

ACTIVITY
1

NAVIGATION AND AVIATION

Overview

As a review of navigation, students use laminated state maps to chart course lines between airports. Using circular protractors, they determine flight directions and calculate flight distances and times. They discover mathematical relationships between the degree measures for initial and returning flights. Working in pairs, students prepare a detailed flight plan to satisfy criteria for a 1,000-mile journey in a Cessna 172, incorporating a head wind and a tail wind. Finally, they examine an aeronautical sectional chart to locate familiar landmarks and to interpret symbols.

Time. Two to three 40- to 50-minute periods.

Purpose. Students review the process of charting an aeronautical course. They recognize the importance of angle measurement to convey an airplane's position. Students apply various strategies to submit a flight plan for the fastest 1,000-mile journey. They realize how wind conditions affect the direction and speed of an airplane. Students also compare charting a course on a state map to using an aeronautical sectional chart.

Materials. *For each student:*
◆ Student Sheets 1.1–1.3
◆ Circular protractor

For each pair of students:
◆ Laminated state map
◆ Ruler
◆ Overhead transparency pens
◆ Calculator
◆ Spray bottle
◆ Rag or sponge
◆ Yardstick
◆ Aeronautical sectional chart

For the teacher:
◆ Aeronautical chart for display
◆ Transparencies of Student Sheets 1.1–1.3 (optional)
◆ Transparency Master 1.4
◆ Blank transparency

Getting Ready

1. Acquire aeronautical charts and state maps.

2. Laminate state maps.

3. Locate circular protractors, rulers, overhead transparency pens, calculators, spray bottles, sponges, and yardsticks.

4. Fill spray bottles with water.

5. Display aeronautical sectional chart.

6. Duplicate Student Sheets 1.1–1.3.

7. Prepare Transparency Master 1.4.

8. Prepare transparencies of Student Sheets 1.1–1.3 (optional).

Background Information

In the Wind is a continuation of the MESA module *In the Air,* which addresses these three basic problems of navigation.

1. How do you determine position?

2. How do you determine which direction to proceed to get to another position?

3. How do you determine distance and the related factors of time and speed?

In the Wind expands these ideas to explore the wind's effect on flight and navigation calculations. Activity 1 highlights techniques and concepts developed in *In the Air.* For students who completed that module, some aspects of Activity 1 will be a review. Depending on your class, students who have not experienced the first module may benefit from doing some or all of the recommended activities in lieu of Student Sheets 1.1–1.2 and before beginning Student Sheet 1.3. Recommended activities from *In the Air* include Student Sheets 2.2, 3.2, 3.3, 3.4, 4.1, and 4.2.

Navigation means knowing where you are and determining a course to where you want to go. Student Sheet 1.1 reviews this concept. Students are given information regarding the location of a house. They are to decide when enough information is given to find a house while they explore the basic components of navigation: destination, distance, and direction.

To navigate, a pilot must have the proper map or chart. An aeronautical chart is a representation of a portion of the earth's surface showing many of the same features as a road map, but it has been specifically designed for convenient use in navigation. It is intended to be worked upon, not merely looked at, and should readily permit the graphic solution of navigational problems, such as the calculations of distance and direction.

Aeronautical charts emphasize or exaggerate landmarks and other features of special importance to pilots, such as tall structures, geographical features, and roads. For example, yellow areas indicate cities, green indicates hillsides, brown denotes mountains, and magenta is used for roads. The intensity in color corresponds to an altitude increase. Because of this added information, aeronautical charts appear cluttered and complicated at first sight. For this reason, students use state maps rather than aeronautical charts throughout this module, but you should display at least one aeronautical chart prominently in the classroom for discussion and comparison.

King of the Road Maps sell current state maps at $0.66 each for orders of at least 100 (see Resources List on page xiv). If you call them two to four months in advance, they may have the maps you require in old stock. These are free. Remember not to submit your request during the summer, because that is their busiest time. Laminating the maps makes them reusable for subsequent classes. Students can use overhead transparency pens to easily alter or emphasize course lines.

Aeronautical charts, known as sectionals, are updated and revised every six months. All obsolete charts are instantly recycled. Teachers can order recycled sectionals from the distribution division of the National Oceanic and Atmospheric Administration (NOAA). (See the Resources List on page xiv). These are often free or at most $2.00 per chart. A letter stating the chart is for classroom use should accompany each request. Make inquiries several months in advance to ensure delivery.

A compass rose oriented toward the north for determining direction is printed on every map or chart. This symbol can be as simple as a single arrow pointing north, or it may be a complete circle divided into compass points and perhaps indicating degree markings from 000° to 360°. In navigation, a compass heading is expressed as an angle in degrees from 000° to 360°. Direction is always expressed in three digits and is read clockwise from true north. A direction 5° northeast is expressed as 005°, and one 35° northeast is 035°. True north may be considered as either 000° or 360° depending on the situation. (See *In the Air,* pages 20–21 and 26–27.)

On all charts, north is a unique direction everywhere on the chart, and on almost all charts, north is toward the top of the page. Finding the direction from one point to another means finding out how many degrees to rotate clockwise from north in order to face the desired direction.

The graphic illustrates one way to do this. Draw a line north from the starting point A and a course line that runs from this point to the destination B. One method to place an accurate north line from any location on the map is to use a ruler and a yardstick or two rulers as a T-square. Then use a circular protractor to measure the angle between the course line and north. Three-inch diameter circular protractors can be purchased for $1.00 each from the C-Thru Ruler Company (see Resources List on page xiv). Also refer to *In the Air* pages 34 and 42.

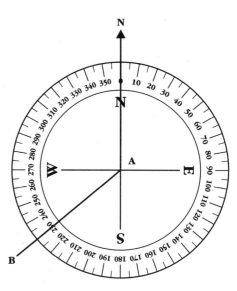

Since all maps are based on true north, pilots determine course directions from true north, and then adjust their compass headings according to the magnetic variation in that area. (See *In the Air* page 4 for more information on magnetic north.) A pilot in Los Angeles adds ⁻014° to the true course; whereas a pilot in Philadelphia adds 010°. The variation in Oregon and Washington is about ⁻020°. Adjusting the course headings for magnetic variation in these activities is not necessary nor recommended. Simply being aware of the phenomenon is sufficient.

One way to calculate the distance between your current location and intended destination on a chart is to measure the length of the course line and use the indicated scale to convert to miles. On most state maps, the scale is in inches. For example, on a Washington State map, 1 inch is equivalent to 14.9 miles. (Other state maps may be scaled differently.) A course line between airports near Seattle and Richland on the Washington state map measures 11.25 inches. Therefore, it is 11.25 × 14.9 = 167.6 miles between Seattle and Richland. (See *In the Air* page 36.)

It is important to properly label all course lines plotted on a chart. By using standardized methods, the plot will mean the same thing to all navigators who read it. The rules for labeling a course line follow.

1. The label for the true course (the direction) is the letter C followed by the degrees and an arrow indicating the direction of the motion. It is placed above an east/west course and to the right of a north/south line.

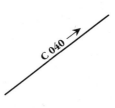

2. Distance is labeled on the other side of the course line with the letter D followed by the distance in miles, to the nearest tenth of a mile.

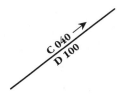

Because pilots generally fly from airport to airport, it is important to note the number of airports throughout the state and their locations. Airplane symbols are used to represent airports. On a Washington State map, there are more than 100 of them noted.

On Student Sheet 1.2, students chart course lines and discover a mathematical relationship between a compass heading in one direction and the compass heading for the return trip. For example, a compass heading of 240° has a return compass heading of 060°. The return direction is always 180° greater or less than the initial direction.

Students learn that the same compass heading from two different locations results in parallel courses. Within the middle latitudes, which includes the continental United States, flying a given course from two different locations generates essentially parallel paths. Though meridians converge at the north pole, on a state map they appear parallel. If two pilots fly north departing from different locations on a 000° course, they are considered to be flying essentially parallel courses that would intersect at the north pole. The greatest convergence occurs above the Arctic Circle and in Antarctica. Courses with the same direction are not considered parallel in these vicinities.

Air navigation is not limited to the actual guiding of an airplane from one place to another—it begins on the ground. This planning phase is called dead reckoning. Dead reckoning is navigating an airplane solely by computations based on airspeed, course, heading, and elapsed time. Pilots determine a course line, allow for wind direction and speed, derive a heading and a ground speed, and estimate time of arrival.

Student Sheet 1.3 presents criteria for students to follow while using dead reckoning to prepare a flight plan for a cross-country journey in a four-seater Cessna 172. A Cessna 172 travels 110–145 knots (approximately 126–167 mph). It holds up to 40 gallons of fuel and uses anywhere from 6–14 gallons per hour. A pilot assumes that a Cessna 172 averages 8 gallons per hour, but to insure she doesn't run out of gas, she considers a full tank of fuel to be equivalent to 4.5 hours of flying time.

Using laminated state maps, students determine airport locations, course directions, and distances. They incorporate actual departure and arrival times based on use of speed, time, and distance relationships. They determine rates of fuel consumption and how to minimize the effects of a head wind and a tail wind on total flight time.

When driving a car for an hour at 60 mph, you can be fairly certain you will travel 60 miles during that hour. An airplane, however, is carried along with movements of the air in which it flies. Because the air is nearly always in motion, the speed of the plane with respect to the ground may be either more or less than the indicated airspeed.

An airplane flying east at an airspeed of 150 mph in still air will have a ground speed of 150 mph. If the mass of air is moving east at 20 mph, the speed of the airplane through the air will not be affected, but the speed of the plane measured with respect to the ground will be 150 mph plus 20 mph—a ground speed of 170 mph. On the other hand, if the mass of air is moving west at 20 mph, the airspeed of the plane still remains the same but the ground speed becomes 150 mph minus 20 mph or 130 mph. This is illustrated on Transparency Master 1.4.

Before departure, a pilot files a flight plan with the Federal Aviation Administration. The flight plan below represents a possible scenario for a 1,000-mile journey in Washington State that meets the criteria listed on Student Sheet 1.3. It is customary to round distances to the nearest tenth of a mile, time to the nearest minute, and compass headings to the nearest degree. Fuel usage is rounded up to tenths, and both air and ground speed are given to the nearest whole number.

The flight time indicates the actual time in the air for each leg of the 1,000-mile journey. The first leg of the flight measures 18.5 inches on a Washington State map with a scale of 1 inch equals 14.9 miles. This converts to 275.6 miles. At an airspeed of 130 mph, the computed flight time using $T = \frac{D}{S}$ is 2.12 hours. Since there are 60 minutes in an hour, the actual flight time is 2 hours + 0.12 × 60 minutes = 2 hours 7 minutes.

The second leg measures 21.5 inches, which is equivalent to 320.4 miles. When computing the flight time for leg two, the ground speed of the plane is 180 mph (130 mph + 50 mph) as a result of the tail wind. Therefore, $\frac{320.4}{180}$ = 1.78 hour or 1 hour 47 minutes. The calculations for leg 3 are similar to those for the first leg. Because of the 25-mph head wind in effect during the fourth leg, the ground speed of the plane is 105 mph for half of the distance and 130 mph for the other half. The flight time for the total distance, 44.7 miles is $\frac{22.35}{105} + \frac{22.35}{130}$ = 0.21 hour + 0.17 hour = 0.38 hour = 23 minutes.

Flight Plan

Depart Time	Location	Destination	Course Heading	Distance (Miles)	Fuel* Usage	Flight Time	Arrival Time
9:00 A.M.	Pasco	Clallum Bay	302°	275.6	40* / 17	2 h 7 min	11:07 A.M.
11:22 A.M.	Clallum Bay	Spokane	100°	320.4	23 / 14.2	1 h 47 min	1:09 P.M.
1:24 P.M.	Spokane	Seattle	269°	225.0	40* / 13.8	1 h 44 min	3:08 P.M.
3:23 P.M.	Seattle	Olympia	222°	44.7	26.2 / 3.0	23 min	3:46 P.M.
4:01 P.M.	Olympia	Pasco	106°	182.5	23.2 / 11.1	1 h 24 min	5:25 P.M.
* Indicates a stop for refueling.			Total	1,048.2	Total	7 h 25 min	

The average ground speed for the journey is about 141 miles per hour. The total time including stopovers is 8 hours 25 minutes.

Use the Technology Link "The Voyage of *Voyager*" and the Career Link "Airline Pilots" anytime during the activity for added interest.

Presenting the Activity

Navigation. Divide students into small working groups. Four to a group works well for this activity. Students can work in pairs and have discussions as a foursome.

Hand out Student Sheet 1.1. Have students work in their groups to respond to the questions. As you circulate, listen to their responses and how they determine the type of information necessary when giving directions. Encourage them to think of what information they need when the address is unknown.

When they have finished, ask the class which of the three people is most likely to arrive at the correct destination. Many will say the person returning the tool has the better chance because she knows the distance and the direction. List groups' responses to question 4. Responses may include the three basics of navigation: destination, distance to travel, and direction. Ask students what the words *north* and *east* refer to. This should lead to a discussion about compass directions and how and why they are used.

Elicit what students know about navigation. Ask if anyone knows a pilot. Explain that to navigate an airplane, a pilot uses some of the same tools and methods involved in traveling by land. All navigation begins with a starting point. From there, a pilot uses mathematics to calculate the direction and distance to travel. When pilots fly, they give directions in degrees. Pilots use the degrees on a circle, called compass headings, to determine their direction. The number of degrees tells them how far to turn clockwise from true north.

Flight Paths. Give each student a circular protractor to use for measuring direction throughout this module. Use a blank overhead transparency to demonstrate how to draw angles with respect to true north. Explain that direction is always read clockwise from true north. Ask groups to draw various angles representing compass headings, such as 025°, 190°, and 230°. Ask groups to decide how to indicate a course heading of 310°. Demonstrate the result based on their input.

Distribute the state maps, yardsticks, rulers, transparency pens, calculators, sponges, and spray bottles. Explain that a state map provides enough information to accurately chart a flight. Remind them that for visual flight, where the pilot relies on visibility, a pilot travels with a state map as well as the appropriate sectional chart. Discuss the mileage scale and the airplane symbols that represent available airports and airfields throughout the state. Have groups locate and mark several airports on their state maps. Ask them if there is a symbol on the map that indicates direction. Once they conclude north is shown, explain the importance of this symbol, called a *compass rose.*

Distribute Student Sheet 1.2 and explain that it will provide experience in determining the locations of airports in the state, drawing course lines, determining directions, and calculating distances and flight time. Ask students to work in pairs but to prepare their own responses to the questions. As you circulate among groups, be sure students know how to correctly place the circular protractor, for measuring direction with its center aligned on the airport representing the starting point. Students may alter or remove course lines by wiping the map clean with a damp sponge.

At the completion of Student Sheet 1.2, have several students present their methods for calculating the compass heading for a return flight in the opposite direction. Ask the class how many 090° course lines are on a chart. Have students explain their conclusions, and then ask how many 140° course lines are on a chart. When students realize there are an infinite number of 090°, 140°, or x° course lines possible on a chart, ask them how the 090° lines are related. How are the 140° lines related?

At the end of the period, remind students to clean the maps for subsequent classes.

A 1,000-Mile Journey. Ask groups to discuss what pre-flight planning and information a 1,000-mile, cross-country journey requires. Ask groups to discuss what they think this information entails. Reconvene the class and list their responses on the blackboard or overhead. Responses should include, but not be limited to, locating airports near intended destinations, plotting course lines on a chart, determining compass headings between airports, measuring distances, and calculating flight, departure, and arrival times. Tell them pilots refer to this process as dead reckoning—a system of determining where the plane should be on the basis of where it has been. It is literally deduced reckoning. *Deduced* was abbreviated *ded,* and the spelling has become *dead reckoning.*

Distribute Student Sheet 1.3, and materials used for Student Sheet 1.2. Students work in pairs and submit a flight plan based on dead reckoning for a 1,000-mile journey throughout the state in a Cessna 172. Describe a Cessna 172 as a four-seater airplane that can travel between 126 mph and 167 mph. Discuss the seven criteria listed for the flight.

Give students time to decide in their groups what effect the 50-mph tail wind will have on the speed of the plane. Solicit ideas and bring out the fact that wind affects the speed of an airplane with respect to the ground. Ask how many miles an airplane flying at an airspeed of 130 mph in still air will cover in one hour. After they conclude it will cover 130 miles over the ground, ask what will happen if there is a 50-mph tail wind. Listen to their group interactions as students conclude that it will actually travel 180 mph over the ground. Refer to this as *ground speed.* Point out that the airspeed indicator in the cockpit will still register that the plane is flying 130 mph. Have each group suggest why this is true. Ask them to decide how a 25-mph head wind will effect the plane if its airspeed is 130 mph. After they conclude that this plane's ground speed reduces to 105 mph, display Transparency Master 1.4 to summarize a similar situation.

Have pairs discuss strategies they might use to complete their journeys in the fastest time. How many different flight paths do they think are possible? Develop the sense that no two flight plans will necessarily be alike.

Emphasize the need to conscientiously check the data for accuracy. Ask students to include their work clearly indicating how they arrived at their distances and flight times for each leg of their journey, especially during wind conditions. Ask, "What could happen if a pilot miscalculated the flight distance?"

As you circulate among the groups to observe and facilitate their work, ask if they can plan a journey that is exactly 1,000 miles and listen to their various strategies for accomplishing this goal. As this activity may span two class periods, be sure students have recorded sufficient information about their flight plans before they clean their maps.

On the second day, while groups are working, ask what information a pilot needs to compute flight time (distance and speed). Ask, "What affects flight time and arrival time? How is arrival time related to departure time?" Establish that departure time is completely independent of flight time; whereas arrival time is dependent upon both the hour of departure and the flight time.

As pairs complete their intended flight paths, suggest they examine other students' charts for comparison, looking for both similarities and differences. Have students present their procedures for finding the flight time with a head wind that lasts only half the length of their leg four. Since total distances may vary, decide with the class how to determine the fastest journeys. They may suggest using a combination of average ground speed along with how close the journey is to 1,000 miles. Be sure to ask if the fastest journey is the best journey. When might it not be the best plan? Their responses may include adverse weather conditions, busy airways, and crowded airports.

If you have them, distribute an appropriate aeronautical sectional chart to each group. If not, take time for students to observe the chart on display in the classroom. Have groups examine the chart to locate their city and other familiar landmarks. Ask them to discuss some of the information a flight chart provides. Point out the scale, various symbols, and colors used. They may realize the bold numbers such as 10^8 and 6^3 indicate altitude, yellow indicates cities, green is for hillsides, brown denotes mountains, and magenta shows roads. Ask, "How does the chart compare to the laminated state map?" Have them locate the compass rose and compare it to other compass rose styles.

Ask students if their cross-country routes would look the same or different on an actual aeronautical chart. Have them explain possible similarities and differences. How might scale affect the appearance of the flight path?

Discussion Questions

1. If everyone in the room stands and faces the door, are they facing the same direction? Explain your reasoning.

   a. If each person turns clockwise to face in the exact opposite direction, how far has each person turned?

   b. Is each person now facing the same destination? Why or why not?

   c. What does this have to do with flight navigation?

2. Why do directions and headings relate to true north?

3. The distance a person travels is a function of time. Do you agree or disagree with this statement? Explain your reasoning.

4. What strategies might someone use in planning a 1,000-mile journey to increase the chances of being the first to return?

5. A Cessna 172 holds 40 gallons of fuel and averages 8 gallons per hour. Why does a pilot consider a fuel tank to be equivalent to 4.5 hours flying time?

Assessment Questions

1. Speed, time, and distance—if you know any two of these, explain how you can find the third.

2. During a 600-mile flight, a pilot maintained a constant course at an airspeed of 150 mph. For 2.4 hours, the pilot encountered a 30-mph head wind.

   a. How did this affect the arrival time?

   b. If the plane departed at 9:00 A.M., what was its arrival time?

   c. How long was the flight?

3. If there is a 50-mph tail wind that lasts for 30 minutes on the second leg of your 1,000-mile journey, determine its effect on the flight time.

4. What effect does the 25-mph head wind on the fourth leg of your 1,000-mile journey have on the flight time if it is in effect for a fourth of the distance?

The Voyage of *Voyager*

For the activities in this module, you are flying a Cessna 172. You have to stop every four hours or so to refuel, so your course is limited to trekking from airport to airport.

But what if you did not have to stop to gas up? What if you could travel the entire 1,000-mile journey without landing? You would save a lot of time! Can you do this in a Cessna? No. But you could do it in *Voyager*, an experimental airplane built in the 1980s. *Voyager* not only went 1,000 miles without landing, it went all the way around the world without landing!

The idea for *Voyager* began as a sketch on a napkin. Its designer, Burt Rutan, was having lunch with friends who wanted to set a new flying record. Lots of people had set records for flying fastest around the world, but no pilot ever flew the entire 25,000 miles without stopping.

The finished plane looked somewhat like a giant H with a long cockpit running through the center. The plane was basically an enormous fuel tank. Even its long wings carried some of the 1,240 gallons of gasoline needed to propel the plane around the world.

Jeana Yeager and Rutan's brother piloted the famous flight in 1986. Nine days after takeoff, *Voyager* touched down again. *Voyager* not only went around the world, it went into history books as one of the world's most famous airplanes.

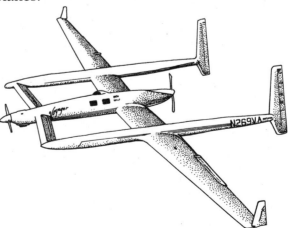

Airline Pilots

Imagine yourself as a captain for a major airline. Before you climb into the cockpit, you carefully plan the flight, inspect the engine and instruments, and make sure the baggage has been loaded correctly.

As the copilot watches the instrument panel, you taxi to the runway and radio the tower. You know the speed the aircraft needs to reach in order to take off by calculating the wind speed, temperature, weight of the plane, elevation of the airport, and other factors. As you zoom down the runway, the copilot tells you the moment the plane reaches takeoff speed. You pull back on the controls and lift the nose of the plane. It zooms up into the sky.

To become a pilot, you first received your bachelor's degree in aviation flight technology. You received your pilot's license with certificates for commercial instrument, multiengine, and flight ratings. You also had to pass a strict physical exam to work as a professional pilot.

There are many advantages to your job. The pay is excellent. As a captain for a major airline, you could earn more than $100,000 a year after some work experience. You and your family also receive free air travel to many places in the world.

However, there are some disadvantages. Planes leave at all hours of the day and night. If you are a newer employee, you do not get to choose your flights on the schedule. So you often work irregular hours. Sometimes you work more than 12 hours a day and then have 9 hours off in whatever city your last flight ended.

If imagining yourself as a pilot sounds exciting, maybe you should explore piloting as a career possibility!

Navigation

Navigation means knowing where you are and how to determine a course to where you want to go.

1. Can someone correctly locate a friend's house if she knows it is one block from her house? Why or why not?

2. Can someone deliver a paper to the correct house if he knows it is east of his house? Why or why not?

3. Can someone return a tool to a neighbor if she knows he lives two blocks north of her house? Why or why not?

4. If you are giving someone directions, what kind of information should you include?

© Washington MESA. Published by Dale Seymour Publications®

Flight Paths

Flying involves knowing where you are, where you want to go, which way to go, and how fast you are going.

1. With your partner, choose an airport on the state map to begin your journey and mark its location with a point. Draw a direction arrow from your departure point that represents true north. Use the indicator for north on your map as a guide.

2. Select another airport in the state as your destination. Draw a course line connecting the two airports.

3. Measure the angle the course line makes with true north to determine your course heading and direction of flight.

4. Complete the flight plan for a Cessna 172 flying at an airspeed of 150 mph. Label the course line with the direction on top and the distance below.

	Departure Location	Destination	Course Heading	Distance	Flight Time
Initial Flight					
Return Flight					

5. Are the initial flight and return flight directions the same? Why or why not?

6. Are the initial flight and return flight distances the same? Why or why not?

Flight Paths

7. When might the initial flight and return flight times for nonstop flights be different? Explain your thinking.

8. If you depart on a course heading of 125°, what course heading should you follow to return home on this same flight path? Draw a diagram to explain your reasoning.

9. If you depart on a course heading of 200°, what course heading should you follow to return home on the same flight path? Explain your reasoning.

10. Locate three other airports on your state map. Chart a 030° course line from each airport and extend them for 150 miles.

    a. How are the three course lines related?

    b. Where will the course lines intersect?

A 1,000-Mile Journey

Before starting a cross-country flight, the pilot plans the journey thoroughly. This includes plotting the course on a chart, measuring distances, allowing for wind conditions, as well as computing course headings, flight time, fuel usage, and estimated time of arrival.

    Be the first to return from a 1,000-mile journey around the state! With your partner, chart a course and record the flight plan for a cross-country flight in a Cessna 172 meeting the following criteria.

1. Airspeed is 130 mph.

2. Departure time is 9:00 A.M.

3. You must land at least four times at different airports before returning. You must remain on the ground for at least 15 minutes at each stop.

4. The total trip must be at least 1,000 miles.

5. Your journey must begin and end at the same location.

6. Wind conditions are forecast as follows: Throughout the second leg, you will encounter a 50-mph tail wind. Expect a 25-mph head wind on the fourth leg for half the distance.

7. You may refuel only once. A Cessna 172 holds 40 gallons of fuel and averages 8 gallons per hour.

A 1,000-Mile Journey

Flight Plan

Depart Time	Location	Destination	Course Heading	Distance (Miles)	Fuel* Usage	Flight Time	Arrival Time
1. 9:00 A.M.					40*		
2.							
3.							
4.							
5.							
6.							

* Indicates a stop for refueling.   Total [   ]   Total [   ]

Average ground speed for the journey is _____.

Total time including stopovers is _____.

Where did you have lunch? _____

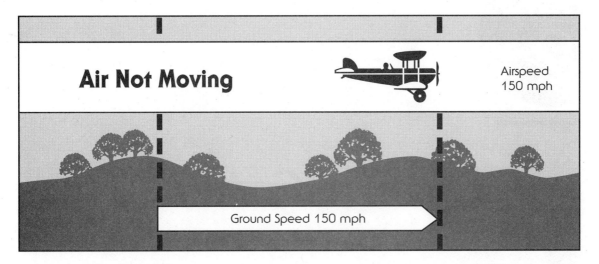

Air Not Moving

Airspeed 150 mph

Ground Speed 150 mph

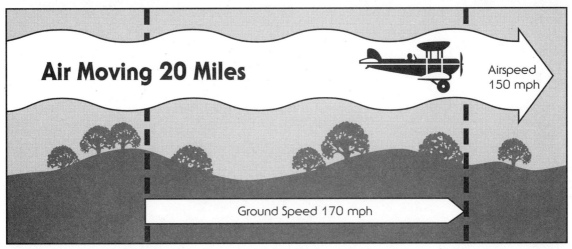

Air Moving 20 Miles

Airspeed 150 mph

Ground Speed 170 mph

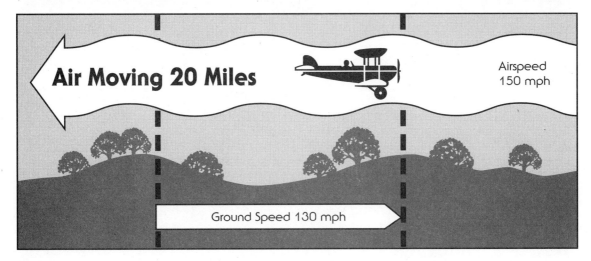

Air Moving 20 Miles

Airspeed 150 mph

Ground Speed 130 mph

ACTIVITY
2

DRIFTING APART

Overview

Students discover the path an airplane follows when continuously pushed off course by wind. They recognize how slight to moderate changes in compass headings might affect their locations. Using scale drawings on grid paper, students simulate aeronautical experiences as they extend course lines to examine the relationship between the distance traveled on an incorrect heading and the number of miles a pilot is off course. The concept of *drift angle* is introduced.

Time. One or two 40- to 50-minute periods.

Purpose. Students realize how wind conditions affect the direction of an airplane in flight. They distinguish between the intended true course of an airplane and the actual path it travels with respect to the ground— its *ground track*. They begin to comprehend the reasons for and the significance of deviations in compass direction. Geometric representations provide a means for collecting and interpreting data regarding flight paths as they discover aspects of the mathematics pilots use to determine their positions when they are off course.

Materials. *For each student:*

◆ Student Sheets 2.1–2.3

◆ Ruler

◆ Circular protractor

◆ Copy of History Link "Amelia Earhart" (page 30)

◆ Copy of Interest Link "What if You Are Off Course?" (page 31)

For each pair of students:

◆ Calculator

◆ Grid paper

◆ Marks-A-Lot® pen

For the teacher:

◆ Transparencies of Student Sheets 2.1–2.3 (optional)

◆ Transparency Master 2.4

Getting Ready

1. Locate rulers, circular protractors, calculators, grid paper, and Marks-A-Lot® pens. Grid paper can be copied from pages 141 and 142.

2. Duplicate History Link and Interest Link.

3. Duplicate Student Sheets 2.1–2.3.

4. Prepare Transparency Master 2.4.

5. Prepare transparencies of Student Sheets 2.1–2.3 (optional).

Background Information

One common form of navigation is known as *pilotage*. After charting a course between two airports, pilots study various landmarks along the route. They identify objects such as water towers, railroads, and power lines that are distinct from the air. They then compute the distance to these landmarks, and knowing the airspeed, make a landmark-to-landmark table, always keeping a known point in view. In actual flight, wind may cause an airplane to deviate considerably from the desired course. The wind may push the plane off the intended course line, and the compass alone will not record this fact. Correction is necessary to keep the plane on its true course. An airplane flying in a moving mass of air will move with the air at the same direction and speed the air is moving with respect to the ground. Consequently, at the end of the given time period the plane will be in a position that results from a combination of two motions: the movement of the air mass with respect to the ground and the forward movement of the airplane through the air mass due to the force of the engine and compass direction. The resulting course of the plane is called the *ground track*—the movement of the plane with respect to the ground.

The diagram below illustrates what happens to an airplane continuously pushed off its 090° course heading by wind onto a series of parallel, 090° headings. Though the nose of the plane continues to face a 090° heading, the plane follows a diagonal path due to the force of the wind.

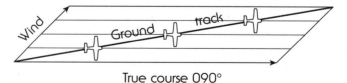

True course 090°

On Student Sheet 2.1, students explore the combination of these forces. Students simulate a flight that has a true course of 090° with a prevailing, due-north wind.

On one sheet of grid paper, pairs of students chart a 10-unit, 090° course and a 10-unit wind arrow of 000° depicting a wind blowing north.

They next draw a 10-unit, 090° course line from the edge of a second sheet of grid paper.

They then align the two 090° course lines with the second sheet of paper on top and the arrow pointing north still visible.

After pairs agree on how they will both travel and pull at the same rate, one student travels the top 090° course line with a Marks-A-Lot® marking pen (which will bleed through to the bottom sheet) while the other student gently pulls the top sheet along the north arrow at the same rate.

When they complete their journey, that is, reach the end of the course line, they remove the top sheet of paper and investigate the ground track—the path they actually flew. They discover the ground track is midway between the 090° course line and the 000° wind arrow. The ground track is actually a 045° course.

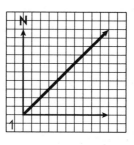

Pilotage is particularly difficult when flying over large bodies of water. Some people believe a navigation error caused Amelia Earhart's mysterious disappearance over the Pacific Ocean. More information on what might have happened appears in the History Link "Amelia Earhart."

The distance off course is related to both the amount of deviation from the desired compass heading, referred to as the *drift angle,* and the distance traveled. Student Sheet 2.2 introduces these concepts by having students prepare scale drawings representing different amounts of drift. The distance off course is measured for various distances traveled, and students discover that the distance off course is not constant—it is a function of the distance traveled. That is, the further one travels off course, the farther away one becomes from the true course.

Students' investigations begin with measuring distances off course for a 60° drift angle. As illustrated, the line segments representing the distance flown off course and the distance intended to fly on the true course at each interval complete equilateral triangles. Therefore, in this case, the distance flown and the miles off course are equivalent. Notice the series of nested similar triangles.

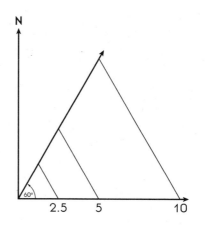

Students observe that as the distance flown doubles, the distance off course also doubles.

On Student Sheet 2.3, students analyze a similar situation with a drift angle of 30°. Based on their measurements, they will verify that as the distance flown doubles, the distance off course also doubles.

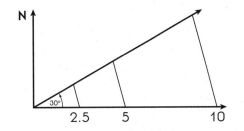

Both of these examples are illustrations of the Midpoint Connector Theorem, which states that the segment connecting the midpoints of two sides of a triangle is parallel to and half the length of the third side. For example, if a pilot has flown for two hours on the wrong course, the plane will be twice as far off course as it was one hour ago, and it will be twice the distance off in four hours as it was in two hours.

Based on these two examples, students may hypothesize that the distance off course for a 30° drift angle is approximately half that for a 60° drift angle, and they may generalize that the distances off course for a drift angle of 20° will be approximately one-third of those with a 60° error. Although these are reasonable estimations, they are in fact not the exact distances off course. It is, however, possible to determine the exact measurements using trigonometry. The actual distances off course can be shown to be close to but not equivalent to these estimations. In addition, it becomes clear that as the distance flown increases, this method of estimation becomes less reliable.

In effect, the angle of deviation is a central angle in a circle whose radius is equal to the distance flown. The chord connecting the endpoints of the arc represents the length of the distance-off-course segment. This is partially illustrated here, showing 30° and 60° angles within arcs of circles whose radii equal the distances flown. The triangles formed by the chord and the two radii are isosceles triangles. The length of a chord with a central angle of $x°$ is equal to $2r \sin \frac{x}{2}$, where r is the radius of the circle.

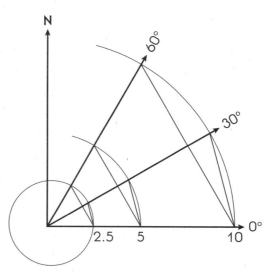

Using this application of sines, the table below contains the calculations for the lengths of the chords in the illustration above and for a potential 20° drift angle. Student measurements on Student Sheets 2.2 and 2.3 will approximate these results.

Lengths of Chords Based on Central Angles

Radius	Central Angle Measures (Drift Angles)		
	60°	30°	20°
2.5	2.5	1.29	0.86
5	5	2.59	1.73
10	10	5.18	3.47
20	20	10.35	6.95

Pilots follow several different actions when unsure of the airplane's position while using pilotage or dead reckoning. The best choice depends upon the circumstances, but usually pilots continue to fly the true course, using recognizable landmarks and wind speed to calculate their drift angles. An explanation of how this is done is given in the Interest Link "What if You Are Off Course?" This link emphasizes how the mathematics of drift angles applies in a real situation. Be sure to use this link at some point in the activity.

Presenting the Activity

Plane Tracks. Divide students into small working groups. Four to a group works well for this activity. Students can work in pairs and have discussions as a foursome.

Find out if students have ever done an activity, such as skateboarding or biking, in which wind has been a contributing factor. Allow time for them to share their experiences. As you distribute Student Sheet 2.1, explain that they are going to explore the effect of wind on an airplane's course.

Give pairs of students two sheets of grid paper, a ruler, a circular protractor, and a Marks-A-Lot® pen. As you circulate among groups, ensure students have devised a strategy that allows them to travel and pull at the same rate. Suggest they practice until they can move at the same rate and accomplish their goal.

When the work is completed, orchestrate a class discussion where students share their results and conclusions about the effects of wind on the path of an airplane. Listen for their understanding of the plane continuing to fly on a 090° course heading while being continuously pushed off course and toward the north by the wind. Have students describe the expected ground track for this plane based on the wind.

Catch My Drift? Ask the class what they know about Amelia Earhart's attempted flight around the world in 1937. Have students read the History Link "Amelia Earhart," then display Transparency Master 2.4, which depicts a possibility in this ill-fated adventure. Point out that Earhart landed on New Guinea and intended to fly to Howland, but never arrived. Elicit possible causes for Earhart to end up on Nikumaroro instead of Howland. List ideas on the overhead. Be sure miscalculations, compass error, wind, and chart misreading are included in the possibilities. Explain that these factors will now be explored in more detail by simulating such flight situations with scale drawings on grid paper.

Distribute Student Sheet 2.2, grid paper, a circular protractor, and a ruler to each student. Circulate among groups to ensure students understand the difference between the true course and the ground track. Elicit their definitions of *drift angle,* and facilitate further group discussion if necessary. Observe their processes as they discover and verify the relationship between the distance traveled and the miles off course.

When the work is completed, orchestrate a class discussion on how the distance off course changes as an airplane continues traveling on an incorrect heading. Focus a discussion on the triangle formed by these three segments: a) the intended distance on the true course, b) the miles flown on the ground track, and c) the distance off course. Elicit the drift angle and determine with your class that the remaining two angles of the triangle must be equal since the lengths marked off define an isosceles triangle. As they conclude that these angle measures must also be 60°, many will realize this triangle is, in fact, equilateral. Thus, for a 60° drift angle, the distance off course is equivalent to the actual distance flown. Students will also notice that the segments representing the distances off course for a 60° drift angle are parallel to each other.

For further emphasis, pose the following situation. What happens if a pilot thinks the plane is on a 090° heading, but in fact it is following a 000° course? How many degrees off course is this plane? Would this be a significant error in navigation? You might ask, "If an airplane leaves San Francisco for Washington, D.C., intending to be on a 090° course, but actually flies on a 000° heading, where would it be 3,000 miles later?" This plane would be near the North Pole, about 4,200 miles off course! This represents an extreme deviation from the intended course line. Verify that the class has a sense of the effects caused by even slight deviations in the compass heading as the distance traveled increases.

Degrees of Drift. Distribute Student Sheet 2.3 with grid paper, rulers, circular protractors, and calculators. As you circulate, remind groups of their observations on Student Sheet 2.2. This may help them determine a drift angle for question 3.

When they have finished, have groups present pertinent aspects of this activity. Give special attention to the basis for their distances-off-course predictions knowing the distances flown and the drift angles. Provide time to consider methods for determining and verifying possible drift angles for the situation in question 3.

If students have not already asked, pose the question, "How do pilots know they are off course? How do they know how far off course?" Hand out the Interest Link "What if You Are Off Course?" and use it as a basis for a discussion.

This activity focuses on the significance of discrepancies between the desired true course and the actual ground track based on possible drift angles. Subsequent activities deal with methods for correcting it.

Discussion Questions

1. What conditions might affect the course of an airplane?

2. What is the distance off course per mile for a 60° drift angle? For a 30° drift angle?

3. Call a pilot or a flight school to find out what drift angles a pilot considers insignificant, and why.

Assessment Questions

1. A plane is flying 40° off course. Explain how to determine the approximate distance off course after 100 miles.

2. Prepare graphs representing the distance flown versus the miles off course for 25° and 45° drift angles. Describe the graphs and write a rule.

3. Use the graphs in question 2 to predict the approximate miles off course an airplane will be after flying 120 miles for each drift angle.

Amelia Earhart

In 1937, Amelia Earhart set out to break another record—to be the first woman to fly around the world. She had already broken four other records. In 1928, Earhart was the first woman passenger to fly across the Atlantic Ocean. The experience prompted her to cross the Atlantic again, this time piloting the plane herself. She accomplished this goal in 1932. Later that year, Earhart became the first woman to fly nonstop across the United States. She was also the first pilot to fly from Hawaii to California.

For her greatest challenge, flying around the world, Earhart and her navigator, Fred Noonan, started in the United States. About 22,000 miles (35,500 kilometers) and several fuel stops later, they successfully reached the island of New Guinea. The next leg of the flight to Howland Island required difficult navigation. On July 2, 1937, Earhart's plane vanished over the Pacific Ocean. It never reached Howland.

In 1992, a group of aircraft archaeologists found evidence Earhart had been forced to down her plane off Nikumaroro, an atoll 420 miles southeast of Howland. The archaeologists found an aluminum map case and a piece of a woman's size 9 shoe, both dating to the 1930s. If the items are really remnants from Earhart's downed plane, a mystery still remains—why were they found 420 miles away from Earhart's route?

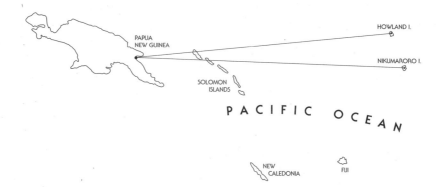

What if You Are Off Course?

When you are flying, you may not realize if the wind has changed speed or direction. What if you are flying your true course and begin to feel you are not where you are supposed to be?

As a pilot, you should constantly verify your position. Watch for landmarks and then recheck your calculated position. Often, the reported wind speed will indicate how many miles you are off course for every hour you fly. For example, if the wind is 20 mph, your plane will be 20 miles off course after an hour of flight.

But what if you do not know in what direction you are off course? First, draw a circle around the point on the map where you should be with a radius equal to the number of miles off course the wind could have pushed you. This is called a *circle of error.*

For example, if you travel 100 miles, and the wind report indicates a 20-mph wind, your plane is about 20 miles off course. You would draw a circle of error as shown.

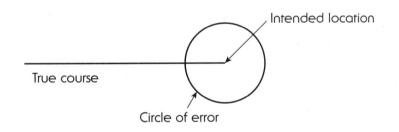

Intended location

True course

Circle of error

You know you are somewhere on the circumference of this circle. Look down to find a familiar landmark. Mark this point on the circumference and draw a line connecting it to the departure point. Now you can measure your drift angle and the actual course you are flying—your ground track. Until you identify a landmark, however, there are an infinite number of possible drift angles!

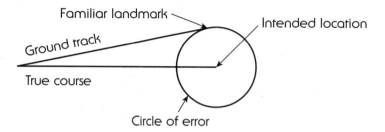

Familiar landmark

Intended location

Ground track

True course

Circle of error

Even if you do not know approximately how many miles you are off course, you should still look for a familiar landmark. Once you see one, mark this point on your chart and connect it with your intended destination point. You now know your distance off course. Connect your position determined by the familiar landmark with your last known checkpoint to find your drift angle.

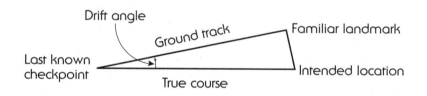

Drift angle

Ground track

Familiar landmark

Last known checkpoint

Intended location

True course

Plane Tracks

1. A pilot is flying at a certain rate on a true course of 090° and the wind is
   blowing 000° due north at the same rate. With your partner, hypothesize
   how you think the plane will actually travel with respect to the ground.
   This is called the *ground track*. Draw the ground track on the diagram.
   Explain your reasoning.

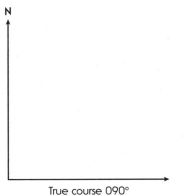

True course 090°

2. Follow these instructions to check your hypothesis.

   a. On a sheet of grid paper, designate a 10-unit, 090° true course and a
      10-unit wind arrow pointing 000° north from the point of departure.

   b. From the edge of a second sheet of grid paper, draw a 10-unit,
      090° course line.

Plane Tracks

   c. Align the two 090° course lines, putting the second sheet of grid paper on top. The arrow pointing north on the bottom sheet should just be visible.

   d. Either you or your partner travel the top sheet's 090° course line with a Marks-A-Lot® pen while the other person gently pulls the top sheet along the north arrow at the same rate. Agree on how you will travel and pull at the same rate.

   e. When you have reached the end of the course line, remove the top sheet of paper.

3. Do the pen tracks on the bottom sheet of grid paper follow the 090° course line? Why or why not?

4. Sketch the track marks with respect to the 10-unit, 090° true course line and the 10-unit wind arrow pointing 000° north. Explain what the pen tracks represent.

Plane Tracks

5. If an airplane is flying at a certain rate on a 090° heading while the wind is blowing toward 000° at the same rate, what course is the plane actually tracking?

6. A plane is flying at a certain rate on a 090° heading while the wind is blowing it toward 000° at a different rate. What effect will the wind have on the plane's course if:

   a. the force of the wind is greater than the airspeed?

   b. the force of the wind is less than the airspeed?

Catch My Drift?

1. Why do you think the number of degrees a pilot is off course is referred to as the *drift angle?*

2. A plane intending to fly on a true course of 090° is actually flying on a ground track of 030°.

   a. Starting near the bottom, left-hand corner of your grid paper, use a circular protractor to chart and label a 090° course line that is 8 inches long.

   b. From the starting point on your grid paper, chart and label a ground track of 030° and extend it for 8 inches.

   c. According to your chart, the drift angle is _____ degrees.

3. As the plane continues on a 030° ground track, will it always be the same distance from the intended 090° course line? Explain your reasoning.

4. Let 1 inch equal 25 miles. Chart and measure the appropriate lengths on the true course and the ground track to determine the approximate distances off course this plane will be after flying 25, 50, 100, and 200 miles. Record your results in the table.

_____ Drift Angle

Miles Traveled	Miles Off Course
25	
50	
100	
200	

Catch My Drift?

5. Predict the approximate distance off course the plane will be after flying 400 miles and after flying 1,000 miles. Explain your reasoning.

6. As the distance this plane travels doubles, the miles off course _____. Explain your reasoning.

Degrees of Drift

1. Another plane intending to fly on a true course of 090° is actually flying on a 060° ground track.

   a. What is its drift angle?

   b. Predict the approximate drift for this plane after 100 miles. Explain your reasoning.

   c. On a sheet of grid paper, chart the true course and the ground track from the same point and extend them for 8 inches. Measure the appropriate lengths on the true course and the ground track to determine the approximate distances off course this plane will be after flying 25, 50, 100, and 200 miles. Record your results in the table, and compare them to your predictions.

   _____ Drift Angle

Miles Traveled	Miles Off Course
25	
50	
100	
200	

   d. As the distance this plane travels doubles, the miles off course _____. Explain your reasoning.

Degrees of Drift

    e. Predict the approximate distance this plane will drift off course after 400 miles and after 1,000 miles. Explain your reasoning.

2. A plane is 20° off course. Predict the approximate drift after 1,000 miles. Demonstrate your reasoning. Test your hypothesis.

3. After traveling 100 miles, an airplane is 20 miles off course.

    a. How many miles will this plane have flown when it is 80 miles off course?

    b. How many miles had it flown when it was 5 miles off course?

    c. Determine a possible drift angle for this flight and demonstrate your process.

4. What drift angles might a pilot consider insignificant? Explain your reasoning.

Drifting Apart

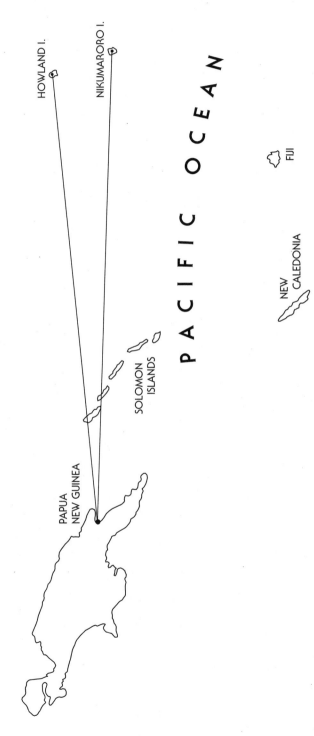

ACTIVITY
3

BLOWING
IN THE WIND

Overview

Students continue to investigate the path an airplane follows as it is continuously pushed off course by wind. Working in pairs, they use tractor-feed strips from used computer paper or Polystrips™ to build models of wind parallelograms which are used to determine the actual flight path. Students investigate the effect wind has on the ground track and ground speed of an airplane, and through this, they are introduced to the concept of vector.

Time. Two 40- to 50-minute periods.

Purpose. Students realize how wind conditions affect the direction and speed of an airplane in flight while they explore the geometry of wind parallelograms. They learn the process pilots use to determine an airplane's ground track and ground speed and to estimate the plane's location, considering both the force of the wind and the speed of the plane.

Materials. *For each student:*

◆ Completed Student Sheet 2.1 (for reference)

◆ Student Sheets 3.1–3.4

◆ Circular protractor

◆ Ruler

For each pair of students:

◆ Calculator

◆ Grid paper

◆ Tractor-feed strips from used computer paper or Polystrips™

◆ 8 brads

For the teacher:

◆ Transparencies of Student Sheets 3.1–3.4 (optional)

◆ Transparency of grid paper

Getting Ready

1. Locate circular protractors, rulers, grid paper, calculators, and brads. Grid paper can be duplicated from pages 141 and 142.

2. Obtain supply of tractor-feed strips from used computer paper or purchase several sets of Polystrips™.

3. Duplicate Student Sheets 3.1–3.4.

4. Prepare transparencies of Student Sheets 3.1–3.4 (optional).

5. Prepare a transparency of grid paper.

Background Information

Pilots will always consult the local Flight Service Station of the National Weather Service Office for preflight weather briefing. The wind speeds and directions pilots use in flight planning are derived from forecast winds. The National Weather Service wind direction forecasts are given in 010° increments. Forecasts can be off as much as 045° before corrections are issued, therefore, pilots must always consider their data approximate.

Weather forecasts give the direction from which the wind is blowing. A wind forecast of 180° is coming from the south and blowing the plane due north toward 000°. For this activity, cardinal directions are used to indicate the direction the wind is blowing in preparation for Activity 4, which introduces wind forecasts in degree measures.

Airspeed indicators are calibrated in knots (nautical miles per hour), and sometimes the miles per hour equivalents are also reported. A knot approximately equals 1.15 mph. Wind speed is only given in knots, and pilots must be sure they are dealing with like units when flight planning. For this module, however, both wind and airspeed are given in miles per hour.

The difference between an airplane's planned course and its track over the ground could be caused by wind drift. If the plane is flying east at an airspeed of 150 mph, and the air mass is moving south at 20 mph, the plane at the end of one hour will be at a point approximately 150 miles east of the departure point due to its progress through the air, and also 20 miles south due to the motion of the wind.

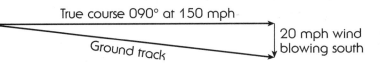

True course 090° at 150 mph

Ground track

20 mph wind blowing south

The explanation of how these forces combine is the mathematics of vectors. Students explore how the different components of vectors combine to determine the path of the plane, but the actual use of vector properties are not introduced until Activity 4.

The true-course vector gives both the direction and speed of the plane. The distance traveled by the plane in one hour is represented by the length of the true-course vector, and the direction the plane is heading is represented by the orientation of the true-course vector. Similarly, the wind vector gives both the direction and speed of the wind. The distance the wind blows the plane in one hour is represented by the length of the wind vector, and the direction toward which the wind is blowing is represented by the orientation of the wind vector. In the example shown, the plane has a true course of 090° with a 150-mph airspeed and the wind is blowing due south at 20 mph.

The plane moves along a series of parallel paths as a result of both forces. It is simultaneously being moved east at 150 mph and south at 20 mph. An observer on the ground sees the plane moving along the diagonal of the resulting parallelogram.

The actual path of the plane is called the *ground track,* and the speed of the plane with respect to the ground is called the *ground speed.* (*Airspeed* refers to the speed of the plane in still air.)

Before pilots depart, they collect weather information, including wind conditions. They use a vector to represent the intended true course and airspeed, and another vector to represent the direction the wind is blowing and the speed of the wind. Using the true-course vector and wind vector as adjacent sides, they complete a wind parallelogram to represent the position of the plane after one hour of flying time. The orientation of the resulting diagonal gives the ground track and the length gives the ground speed. Pilots use wind parallelograms to facilitate these calculations, just as students do in this activity.

Student Sheet 3.1 introduces students to the concept of vectors without using the term. They draw an arrow indicating the distance and direction flown on the true course after one hour, and another arrow indicating the distance and direction the wind has blown after one hour. They complete the wind parallelogram, determine the resulting diagonal, and discuss how it represents the ground track, as well as the location of the plane after one hour of flying in this wind. They determine the direction of the ground track and discuss how one would determine the ground speed.

Pilots use parallel rulers to form wind parallelograms. On Student Sheet 3.2, students will build models of parallel rulers using tractor-feed strips—the narrow strips of paper full of holes that feed computer paper through printers. For a less fragile manipulative, use Polystrips™ (see Resources). One set contains 12 long and 6 short strips and 24 brads, enough for four student pairs. The holes in the tractor strips are punched at 0.5-inch intervals. The holes in the Polystrips™ are punched at 1.5-cm intervals. Students fasten these together to form flexible parallelograms. See Student Sheet 3.2 for a diagram.

The materials used for making the wind parallelograms will determine the scale used throughout this activity. If tractor-feed strips are used, the scale should be 1 unit = 0.5 in = 10 miles; if Polystrips™ are used the scale should be 1 unit = 1.5 cm = 10 miles. Choose the appropriate grid paper; blackline masters for both 0.25-inch and 0.5-centimeter grid paper are included in the back of the book (pages 141–142).

Using a scale of 1 unit equals 10 miles, students make wind parallelograms to represent situations that might arise in normal flight. A Cessna 172 can fly safely in various wind conditions; yet airports will not clear it to land if the cross winds exceed 20 mph. Since strong head winds above 35 mph reduce the ground speed significantly, most pilots choose not to fly under these conditions. However, a 60-mph tail wind would be acceptable.

Because a wind parallelogram is not rigid, it is possible to form an infinite number of different parallelograms by altering either the true course or the wind direction, while keeping both airspeed and wind speed constant. On Student Sheet 3.2, students explore various flight situations in which the airspeed and wind speed remain constant but the direction of either varies. Through this, they might notice there are two components of vectors—speed and direction.

The first graphic represents a plane with a 130-mph airspeed on a 090° true course with a wind blowing due south at 40 mph. The length of the true-course vector represents the airspeed. Since the airspeed is given in mph, the length of the true-course vector also represents the distance the plane intends to travel in one hour. Similarly, the length of the wind vector represents the wind speed, as well as the distance the wind has

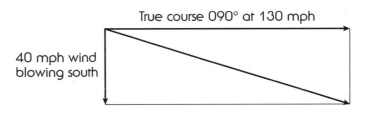

True course 090° at 130 mph

40 mph wind blowing south

blown a particle of air in one hour. The orientation of the true-course vector represents the direction the pilot is heading the plane, and the orientation of the wind vector represents the direction the wind is blowing the plane. The diagonal represents the actual flight path, both the ground track (the direction the plane is moving) and the ground speed (the speed the plane is moving with respect to the ground). The length of the true-course vector is 13 units (1 unit equals 10 mph, so the intended distance traveled in one hour is 130 miles), the length of the wind vector is 4 units, and the length of the diagonal is 13.6 units. In one hour the plane will have actually traveled 136 miles, thus the ground speed is 136 mph.

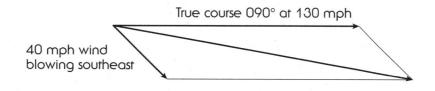

True course 090° at 130 mph

40 mph wind blowing southeast

If either the direction of the wind or the true course change, the actual flight path changes. The second drawing illustrates the same true course as the first, but with a wind blowing southeast. The length of the true-course vector remains 13 units, the length of the wind vector remains 4 units, but the length of the diagonal (the ground-track vector) is 16.1 units. The ground speed is therefore 161 mph.

The third drawing illustrates the same wind direction as in the first but with a true course of 100°, and the ground speed is a little more than 140 mph.

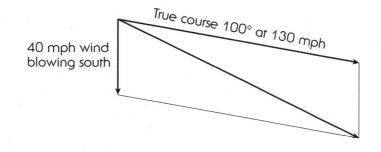

True course 100° at 130 mph

40 mph wind blowing south

This drawing shows the effect of change in both wind and true-course directions, and the ground speed is nearly 165 mph.

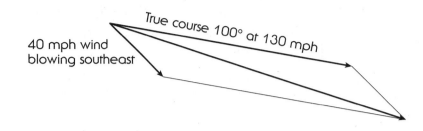

40 mph wind blowing southeast

True course 100° at 130 mph

On Student Sheet 3.3, students construct a series of wind parallelograms in which only the wind direction changes while the wind speed, true course, and airspeed remain unchanged. The diagonals of the wind parallelograms show the actual path over the ground the plane will track due to the combination of the motion of the airplane and the motion of the air. Since the wind parallelograms are built to scale for one hour of flight, students can use the length of the diagonal (the ground track) to determine the rate in miles per hour the plane is actually traveling over the ground (its ground speed). Students analyze how the change in wind direction affects both the ground track and ground speed.

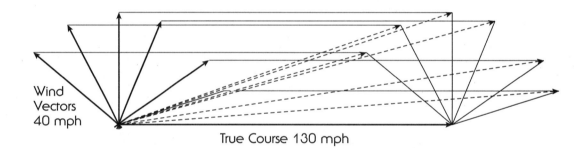

Wind Vectors 40 mph

True Course 130 mph

As the direction of the wind varies from the true course, note the pattern of its effect on the ground track and the resulting ground speed. The greatest positive effect occurs when the wind represents a tail wind, and the ground speed is equivalent to the airspeed plus the wind speed, or 170 mph. In this situation, the true-course and wind vectors are collinear, so they cannot be represented as a parallelogram. This situation, therefore, is not represented in the above illustration.

The positive effect lessens as the wind direction moves in a circular path toward a direction that is perpendicular to the true course. There is a point along this path where the ground speed is equal to the airspeed. This occurs when the true-course vector and ground-track vector are equal in length, and they, along with the wind vector, form an isosceles triangle. In this example, that occurs when the drift angle is about 18°. The plane will have gone 130 miles in one hour, but not in the intended direction.

As the wind direction continues to move in a circular path toward a head wind, the ground speed decreases. It is at its least when the wind is a head wind, when the ground speed is equivalent to the airspeed minus the wind speed, or 90 mph. For a 130-mph airspeed and a 40-mph wind speed, the ground speed ranges from 90 mph to 170 mph.

On Student Sheet 3.4, students construct a series of wind parallelograms in which the wind speed is repeatedly doubled, but the wind direction, true course, and airspeed remain unchanged. They then analyze how a change in wind speed affects ground track and ground speed.

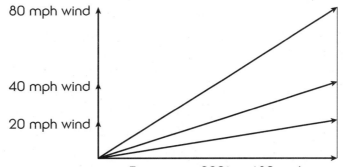

The graphic shows three wind parallelograms in which the true course, airspeed, and wind direction are the same, but the wind speeds differ. Note the patterns of effects on the drift angle. As the wind speed doubles, the drift angle increases, but not quite at the same rate. If the airspeed in the example were 130 mph, then a 20-mph wind blowing north would result in a 9° drift angle, a 40-mph wind blowing north would result in a 17° drift angle, and an 80-mph wind blowing north would result in a 32° drift angle.

The ground speed is also increasing, but it is not doubling. If the airspeed were 130 mph, based on the Pythagorean Theorem, the ground speed would be $(130^2 + W^2)^{1/2}$ with W = wind speed. For W = 20 mph, the ground speed would be about 132 mph; for W = 40 mph, the ground speed would be about 136 mph; and for W = 80 mph, the ground speed would be about 153 mph.

A wind speed of 80 mph might not represent a realistic situation for a Cessna 172, but it is included to illustrate the mathematics of the situation.

The student sheets are designed to facilitate understanding of the two components of vectors, speed and direction, which will be the focus of Activity 4.

Use the Interest Link "Wind" and the Career Link "Meteorologists" at any time during the activity to further student interest.

Presenting the Activity

Windy Conditions. Divide students into small working groups. Four to a group works well for this activity. Students can work in pairs and have discussions as a foursome.

Hand out or have students locate completed Student Sheet 2.1. Allow time for groups to recall and discuss their work. Hand out Student Sheet 3.1 making sure to use the grid paper that is appropriate to the materials the students will use in building their wind parallelograms. If they are going to use tractor feed strips, hand out the 0.25 in grid paper and be sure students understand that two squares on the grid paper is one unit on the tractor-feed strips. As you talk about the scale, emphasize that one-half inch equals 10 miles." If they are going to use Polystrips™, hand out the 0.5-cm grid paper and be sure students understand three squares on the grid paper is one unit. Refer to the scale as one unit equals 10 miles or 1.5 centimeters equals 10 miles. The students will also need rulers.

As you circulate among the groups, ensure that students understand that the ground track is the actual flight path of the plane in relation to the ground, and also listen for their strategies to determine the ground speed.

When the work is completed, have groups share their results with the class. Pursue, along with their thinging on 4.1, how they would find ground speed by plotting arrows on grid paper representing the true course and wind for other flights. Draw their suggestions on an overhead transparency of grid paper.

Have groups share their thinking and conclusions to question 4. Ask how pilots might use wind parallelograms. If mention is made of parallel rulers or some comparable hands-on tool, extend the discussion to pilots' use of these tools. Explain that students are going to build a model of a wind parallelogram using tractor-feed strips or Polystrips™ and brass brads.

Wind Parallelograms. Hand out Student Sheet 3.2, tractor strips or Polystrips™, and brads. Have students work in pairs to build wind parallelograms simulating an airplane flying at an airspeed of 130 mph with a 40-mph wind crossing its path. As you circulate, make sure students understand how to measure length on the tractor strips or Polystrips™—it is the distance between the center of the holes. They need not cut the tractor strips; overhang is fine, and the strips can then be reused to represent different flight situations.

When pairs have built their wind parallelograms, check that they have labeled the sides representing the true course and the wind. If necessary, clarify that the wind parallelogram is defined by the center of the brads and holes, not the edges of the strips. Observe their explorations and note their comments. If you do not hear discussion regarding the differing diagonals in any one group, ask "What did you notice about the diagonals in your investigations?"

Give groups time to discuss their work, then orchestrate a class discussion to allow students to share their observations and conclusions with the class. Focus a class discussion on the infinite number of parallelograms that can be formed with this one wind parallelogram. Make sure students understand that even though the sides of the parallelogram remain constant, the diagonals differ in length as a result of the orientation of the sides. Ask how this information relates to ground track and ground speed.

The information that each side of a wind parallelogram represents both the direction and speed might come out in the discussion, and then again, it might not. Student Sheets 3.3 and 3.4 will emphasize these two components.

Wind Shifts. As you distribute Student Sheet 3.3, tell students they are going to specifically investigate how change in just the direction of the wind affects both the ground track and the ground speed. Hand out circular protractors, rulers, calculators, and grid paper to each pair of students. If students want personal copies of the wind parallelograms, distribute three sheets of grid paper to each student.

As you circulate, make sure students are carefully tracing the wind parallelograms onto the grid paper. Insure that students realize the scale is one unit (0.5 in. or 1.5 cm) equals 10 miles. The endpoint of the wind parallelogram that represents the starting point of the flight must match up with a crosshatch on the grid paper. Suggest one student hold the wind parallelogram in place while the other mark the position of a few holes per edge to accurately copy the parallelogram. Students can then use rulers to connect the markings per side to complete the outlines. Since it is difficult to mark the endpoints because of the brads, students might want to use rulers to check the lengths of each side.

After all students have completed question 4, discuss as a class students' initial predictions on how a change in wind direction affects the ground track and ground speed. Some students might have already started to collect data on these effects. Have them describe what they observe, recognizing that their arguments will be a function of the specific change in wind direction they make and recalling the pattern of effects described in the background information.

If the discussion becomes too divergent, stop it for now, have students complete the entire worksheet, and then continue the discussion using a transparency of grid paper to elicit this pattern of effects from the sum of everyone's work. Have students save or turn in the completed student sheets with graphs attached. They will use them in Activity 5.

Wind Speeds. Distribute Student Sheet 3.4, grid paper, a ruler, and a protractor to each student. Have them work in their groups to complete the wind parallelograms, locate the ground tracks, and determine the ground speeds. While they are working, observe their interactions and procedures. In group discussions, many will hypothesize that as the wind speed is continually doubled, so is the drift angle. Though this is a good approximation, the actual angle measurements require trigonometry. If it has not come up in the discussion, ask the class if they think a Cessna 172 could be flying in an 80-mph wind.

In summary, work through a few student-presented examples as a class so all students understand that it is the combined effects of the plane's direction and speed along with the wind's direction and speed that determine the ground track and resulting ground speed of the plane. Be sure they acknowledge that the ground track corresponds to the diagonal of the parallelogram.

Discussion Questions

1. What factors affect the actual speed of an airplane?

2. How does airspeed compare to ground speed?

3. Flying at 150 mph on a 090° course with a 50-mph wind blowing due south, is the plane flying faster or slower than the intended airspeed? How do you know? After one hour, how far is this plane from the 090° course? Explain your reasoning.

4. If you are intending to fly on a 090° true course, what is the farthest off course the force of a wind can blow you? Explain your reasoning.

5. How can the wind parallelogram be used to represent a wind blowing the plane west? Southwest?

Assessment Questions

1. Explain why a wind parallelogram can be used to determine the actual path of an airplane flying in the wind.

2. A plane departs on a true course of 320° at a speed of 150 mph. Because of the wind, the plane is actually tracking a course of 310° and

has a ground speed of 180 mph. What is the direction and speed of the wind?

3. The diagram represents a ground track and shows the location of the airplane after one hour in flight. With a partner, determine a true course the pilot intended to fly and the direction of the wind blowing the plane off course. Explain your process.

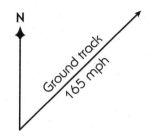

4. After flying on a true course of 060° for one hour at 150 mph, a pilot realizes she has been blown off course by a 20-mph wind. Where is she located?

Wind

What makes the wind blow? To understand the answer, keep in mind this basic principle: warm air rises and expands because when air is warmed the air molecules move faster and spread out. Molecules in cold air move slower and are much more closely packed together. So hot air is less dense and therefore lighter than the same amount of cold air.

As the earth spins, the sun warms some spots on earth more than others. Dark surfaces absorb more of the sun's energy than do light-colored surfaces. As energy is absorbed, the temperature rises. The air above these hot spots rises too, and cool air rushes in to fill the void caused by rising air. This kind of movement is called *convection*.

As convection continues, an area of low pressure forms under the rising warm air. High pressure forms under the sinking cooler air. This difference of density and pressure over continents and oceans, as well as between hot and cold regions, makes the air move and thus starts the winds blowing.

Imagine, for example, the temperature differences between the equator and the poles. As you might expect, the warm air at the equator tends to rise and be replaced by cold air moving in underneath it from the poles. These pressure differences create a general movement of air worldwide.

The earth's rotation also affects the winds. That is why global winds tend to circle around the globe rather than flow in straight lines from the poles to the equator.

Why do you think breezes flow from the sea to the beach during the day, and then from the beach to the sea at night?

Meteorologists

Pilots need current, accurate information about wind, storms, temperature, clouds, and other weather data. Keeping this flow of information coming is the job of meteorologists.

Meteorologists study weather conditions and forecast weather changes. They often use satellites and other specialized equipment to collect data about the atmosphere. They use observations, weather maps, and instrument readings to forecast the weather—a difficult task since weather is so unpredictable and depends upon so many factors.

Pilots are not the only people who need weather information. Ship captains, farmers, astronauts, and many others rely on weather forecasts. Meteorologists also tackle the task of identifying thunderstorms, hurricanes, and tornadoes—with the hope there will be enough time to warn communities before the fierce weather arrives.

Meteorologists may work for the federal government's National Weather Service, for television networks, for universities as teachers, or for private businesses.

To become a meteorologist, you need a bachelor's degree in meteorology. About 100 colleges now offer this major. You can also get graduate degrees and specialize in aspects of meteorology. The armed forces also offers training in meteorology. Salaries range from $20,000 to more than $50,000 a year depending on experience. Supervisors in private industry earn as much as $90,000 a year.

The National Weather Service and National Oceanographic and Atmospheric Administration have volunteer programs for students. This would be a way for you to explore the possibility of a career in meteorology.

Windy Conditions

1. A pilot is flying at a rate of 100 mph on a true course of 090°. Using a scale of 0.5 inches equals 10 miles or 1.5 centimeters equals 10 miles, draw an arrow on grid paper that shows the true course for the first hour.

2. The wind is blowing due north at the same rate. Using the same scale, draw an arrow showing the effects of the wind for the first hour.

3. Draw a line with an arrow that shows the actual flight path of the plane during the first hour. This is called the *ground track*.

4. Complete the parallelogram that has the true course and the wind as sides.

   a. What is the relationship of the ground track to this parallelogram?

   b. Decide if this plane is flying faster or slower than its airspeed of 100 mph. Explain your reasoning.

   c. The ground speed is defined as the plane's speed with respect to the ground. Determine the ground speed. Describe your process.

   d. Discuss with your group why this is called a *wind parallelogram*.

Wind Parallelograms

Pilots use wind parallelograms to understand how wind affects their flight paths. You are going to build a replica of one using tractor-feed strips or Polystrips™ and brads.

1. With your partner, follow these directions to build a wind parallelogram as shown to represent an airplane flying at an airspeed of 130 mph with a 40-mph wind crossing its path.

   a. Let the distance between the centers of adjoining holes represent 10 mph.

   b. Prepare two strips to represent the distance flown after one hour. Label them *true course*.

   c. Prepare two strips to represent the wind speed for that one hour, and label them *wind*.

   d. Attach the strips together with the brads to form a wind parallelogram.

Wind Parallelograms

2. As a group, investigate the possibilities of this wind parallelogram.

    a. How many different parallelograms can you make with your wind parallelogram? Explain your reasoning.

    b. How do the parallelograms differ?

    c. How are they similar?

3. Where is the ground track located on each wind parallelogram?

    a. When does the ground track indicate the plane is flying faster than its airspeed?

    b. When does the ground track indicate the plane is flying slower than its airspeed?

    c. When does the ground track indicate the plane is flying at the same rate as its airspeed?

STUDENT SHEET 3.3

Wind Shifts

1. With your partner, arrange your wind parallelogram to simulate an airplane flying 130 mph on a true course of 180° with a 40-mph wind blowing due east. Trace a copy of your wind parallelogram onto grid paper. Carefully align the endpoints of your parallelogram with the crosshatches on the grid paper, and mark the centers of several holes per side. Connect them with a ruler to complete the outline of the parallelogram. Label the true course, airspeed, wind speed, and wind direction. Indicate and label the ground track.

2. Use your drawing to determine the distance this plane has flown after an hour, its ground speed, the drift angle, and the ground-track direction. Record your data in the table below.

After One Hour	Cardinal Wind Directions			
	East			
Distance Flown				
Ground Speed				
Drift Angle				
Ground Track				

3. Discuss with your group how changes in wind direction will affect the plane's ground track, ground speed, and drift angle. Write your predictions here.

© Washington MESA. Published by Dale Seymour Publications®   BLOWING IN THE WIND   **59**

Wind Shifts

4. Shift your wind parallelogram to demonstrate a situation in which an airplane is flying 130 mph on a true course of 180° with a 40-mph wind blowing in a different cardinal direction, north, south, west, but not east. Trace a copy of this wind parallelogram onto grid paper, again being careful to align the endpoints of your parallelogram with the crosshatches on the grid paper. Label the true course, airspeed, wind speed, and wind direction, then indicate the ground track of the plane. Use your drawing to determine the distance this plane has flown after one hour, its ground speed, ground track, and the drift angle. Record your data in the table above, and compare them to your initial hypotheses.

5. Shift your wind parallelogram to demonstrate another situation, one in which an airplane is flying 130 mph on a true course of 180° with a 40-mph wind blowing in yet another cardinal direction. Trace a copy of this wind parallelogram onto grid paper. Label the true course, airspeed, wind speed, and wind direction, and indicate the actual flight path of the plane. Use your drawing to determine the distance this plane has flown after one hour, its ground speed, ground track, and the drift angle. Record your data in the table above, and compare them to your initial hypotheses.

6. As the direction the wind is blowing approaches 180°, the wind becomes a _____, and the ground speed is _____. Discuss with your group and illustrate how the wind parallelogram might show this.

Wind Shifts

7. As the direction the wind is blowing approaches 000°, the wind becomes
   a _____, and the ground speed is _____. Discuss with your
   group, and illustrate how the wind parallelogram might show this.

8. Based on your data, discuss how wind direction affects the flight path.

Wind Speeds

1. Construct a wind parallelogram, and trace it onto grid paper to simulate an airplane flying 130 mph on a true course of 090° with a 20-mph wind blowing due north. Label the true course, airspeed, wind speed, and wind direction. Indicate and label the ground track.

2. Use your drawing to determine the distance this plane has flown after one hour, its ground speed, and the drift angle. Record your data in the table below.

3. Discuss with your group how doubling the wind speed to 40 mph will affect the ground track, its ground speed, and the drift angle. Write your predictions here.

4. Modify your wind parallelogram for 130 mph true course of 090° to represent a 40-mph wind blowing due north, and indicate the ground track of the plane. Use your drawing to determine the distance this plane has flown after one hour, its ground speed, and the drift angle. Record your data in the table below, and compare the data to your initial hypotheses.

5. Based on your results, discuss with your group how doubling the wind speed again to 80 mph will affect the ground track, its ground speed, and the drift angle. Write your predictions here.

Wind Speeds

6. Modify your wind parallelogram of the same flight to represent an 80-mph wind blowing due north, and indicate the ground track of the plane. Use your drawing to determine the distance this plane has flown after one hour, its ground speed, and the drift angle. Record your data in the table, and compare the data to your initial hypotheses.

	Wind Speeds			
After One Hour	0 mph	20 mph	40 mph	80 mph
Distance Flown				
Ground Speed				
Drift Angle				

7. Discuss with your group what you think the ground speed and drift angle might be for a 60-mph wind. Test your hypothesis.

8. Based on your data, what observations can you make about how wind speed affects the ground speed and the drift angle?

ACTIVITY
4

WHEN THE WIND BLOWS

Overview

Forecast information provides the direction from which the wind is blowing. Students use the forecast data to determine the direction toward which the wind is blowing an airplane. After students are introduced to vectors, they use them to determine the effect wind has on a planned flight course, relating the situations to their previous work with wind parallelograms. Vectors are then applied to establish an airplane's ground track and ground speed.

Time. Two to three 40- to 50-minute periods.

Purpose. Students recognize the relationship between the forecast wind direction and the direction the wind is blowing the plane. They develop a sense of how vector properties can be used to solve navigation problems.

Materials. *For each student:*

◆ Student Sheets 4.1–4.6

◆ Circular protractor

◆ Ruler

For each pair of students:

◆ Calculator

◆ Tractor-feed strips from used computer paper or Polystrips™

◆ 8 brads

◆ Laminated state map

◆ Rag or sponge

◆ Overhead transparency pen

◆ Spray bottle

◆ Yardstick

◆ Grid paper

For the teacher:

◆ Transparencies of Student Sheets 4.1–4.6 (optional)

Getting Ready

1. Locate circular protractors, rulers, grid paper, calculators, tractor-feed strips or Polystrips™, brads, state maps, sponges, transparency pens, spray bottles, and yardsticks. Grid paper can be duplicated from pages 141 and 142.

2. Duplicate Student Sheets 4.1–4.6.

3. Prepare transparencies of Student Sheet 4.1–4.6 (optional).

4. Fill spray bottles with water.

Background Information

Wind direction is reported in relation to true north and always is given as the direction from which the wind is blowing. In order to plot the appropriate wind vector for determining the effect wind has on a true course, a pilot calculates the direction toward which the wind is blowing the plane. For example, if the reported wind direction is 120°, then the wind is blowing from 120°. It is blowing toward 300°, and therefore, is blowing the plane toward 300°. Student Sheet 4.1 expands this idea.

A quantity that has size but no direction, such as volume, is called a *scalar* quantity. A *vector* quantity is something that has magnitude (size) as well as direction. Velocity is an example. When traveling, you need to know how fast you are going as well as in what direction. The scalar quantity speed and a direction combine to form a vector that represents velocity. The idea of using directed arrows to represent vectors is credited to the famous mathematician and scientist Isaac Newton. The length of the line segment drawn to scale represents the magnitude (speed) of the vector quantity, and the orientation of the line segment represents its direction. An arrowhead is used to distinguish the terminal from the initial point.

You can use vector addition to obtain the result of two forces that are simultaneously applied to an object, such as the force of an airplane and the force of the wind. To determine the sum of two vectors, apply the same parallelogram method used to determine the ground track.

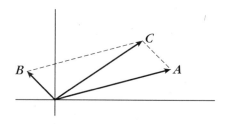

Vectors that have the same length and direction are considered equal. Because of this, you can construct a parallelogram where the resultant diagonal of the parallelogram is the sum of the two vectors.

For example, if you walk 2 miles in a certain direction, then turn northwest and walk another mile, your location can be represented by the vector that begins at the starting point and ends at the final destination. This is called *vector addition.* The sum of the vectors *A* and *B* is defined to be the vector *C* that goes from the tail, or initial point, of the first vector to the head, or terminal point, of the second one.

Vector addition helps solve navigation problems when airplanes travel in moving air. The sum depends on both the direction and the magnitude of the course and wind vectors.

Vectors can be represented geometrically in terms of coordinates. Think of the initial and terminal points of a vector as points in a coordinate system—assign (0, 0) to the initial point of the vector and (*x, y*) to the terminal point. In the example shown, assign (0, 0) as the initial point of both the course vector and the wind vector. Assign (7, 2) as the terminal point of the course vector and (1, 4) as the terminal point of the wind vector. Since vectors with the same length and direction are equal, complete the parallelogram to determine the coordinates for the terminal point of the ground-track vector (8, 6). To find the *x*-coordinate of the ground-track vector's terminal point, add the *x*-coordinates of the true-course and wind vectors (7 + 1 = 8). To find the *y*-coordinate of the terminal point of the ground-track vector, add the *y*-coordinates of the true-course and wind vectors (2 + 4 = 6).

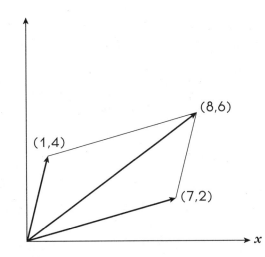

Student Sheet 4.3 introduces vector addition and Student Sheet 4.4 continues to develop the concept. On Student Sheets 4.5 and 4.6, students use vectors to determine the ground track and ground speed in various flight situations.

Using graphical methods to solve vector problems, although suitable in many cases, is not the most accurate approach. However, it is a method available to the pre-trigonometry student. Because of the uncertainty associated with all measurement, results obtained by graphing methods dependent on measurement are only approximate. The parallelogram method of vector addition for a pre-trig student depends on drawing and estimation skill as well as the condition of the measuring tools used. As students continue their study of mathematics, they will find that greater accuracy is achieved by using trigonometric relationships.

Use the Technology Link "Wind Shear" and the Interest Link "Weather Conditions" at any time during the activity to enhance student interest.

Presenting the Activity

Where the Wind Blows. Divide students into small working groups. Four to a group works well for this activity. Students can work in pairs and have discussions as a foursome.

Elicit from the class what they know about weather forecasts, including wind directions. If it does not come out in the discussion, explain that wind forecasts are always reported as the direction from which the wind is blowing. Ask how a pilot might use this information. While handing out Student Sheet 4.1 and the circular protractors, ask students to work in their groups to discover how a pilot determines the direction an airplane is being blown by the wind.

After groups finish, entertain a discussion to clarify the process for determining the direction toward which the wind is blowing the plane. Be sure they recognize that when the given wind is from a direction that is less than or equal to 180°, a pilot adds 180° to the wind direction, but when the direction from which the wind is coming is greater than 180°, a pilot subtracts 180° (or adds ⁻180°).

Parallelogram Plots. Hand out Student Sheet 4.2, tractor strips or Polystrips™, brads, grid paper, rulers, and calculators. Explain to students they are going to build new wind parallelograms and trace them onto grid paper, similar to what they did in Activity 3.

As you circulate, ensure that students are using a scale of 0.5 inches (or 1.5 centimeters) equals one unit equals 10 miles. Observe how groups set up the coordinate axes to accommodate the placement of the wind parallelogram. Everyone should understand that the origin is (0, 0). One unit on the 0.25-inch grid paper is two squares, on the 0.5-centimeter grid paper it is three squares. Also check the starting point of the wind parallelogram, the lower left brad—it should be aligned with (0, 0). Groups should experience little problem with this extension of their work from the last activity.

When all students have completed question 2, orchestrate a class discussion on the coordinate system. Work through the example as a class if you deem it necessary. List responses to question 2d on the blackboard until you have exhausted all the possible things students know about the ground track of the proposed flight. This should include that its direction is about 073°, its length is about 6.75 inches (or 20.25 centimeters), the distance traveled in one hour is about 135 miles, the ground speed is about 135 mph, the ground track is longer than the course vector (indicating the plane is traveling faster than its airspeed), and its terminal coordinates are (13, 4) for a scale of one unit equals 10 miles.

Allow time for students in their groups to develop a concept of vectors. After they have formulated their rationale of why course and wind arrows are called vectors, have groups share their reasoning with the class. Conclude the discussion with their explanation that the ground track is a vector because it has both a direction and a speed.

Vector Ventures. Hand out Student Sheet 4.3 and a sheet of grid paper to each student along with calculators and circular protractors if students do not already have them. Since students are not copying wind parallelograms made from tractor-feed strips onto the grid paper, you can use one unit on the 0.25-inch grid paper to represent ten miles.

As you circulate, ensure that students know how to plot the vector given its terminal coordinates. As a conclusion, allow students to share their thinking with the class. Ensure that everyone understands the two components of each of these vectors, including the ground-track vector.

Sum Vectors. Hand out Student Sheet 4.4 and grid paper to each student. Students also need rulers and circular protractors. Explain to students they are going to continue graphing wind parallelograms and investigate some of the mathematical properties of vectors. Since they will be adding information to their graphs in Activity 5, suggest they draw one graph to a sheet. Observe as groups work to see that they clearly label their graphs for easy reference in the next activity.

After they finish question 2, conduct a class discussion to highlight the addition process to locate the ground-track vector. The discussion should include the relationship between the x-coordinates of the course, wind, and ground-track vectors, as well as the relationship between the analogous *y*-coordinates. Some may realize that adding the corresponding terminal coordinates of a true-course vector and the wind vector together provides another way to locate the terminal point of the ground-track vector without drawing the wind parallelogram. If it does not arise in the discussion, ask if it would be possible to determine the ground-track vector without drawing the parallelogram.

Have students resume work on question 3. If you observe groups struggling to determine a true-course and a wind vector for a ground track whose terminal coordinates are (12, 7), provide them a set of terminal coordinates for the true-course vector, such as (4, 11), and ask them what they would then know about the wind.

After groups have had time to resolve question 3, have them present their solutions to the class. If you think some students do not fully comprehend there are an infinite number of course and wind vector combinations that satisfy the given ground-track situation, follow up with a different set of coordinates for the true-course vector, and have students determine the appropriate terminal coordinates for the wind vector. It will become clear there is no unique solution. An infinite number of course and wind vector combinations satisfy the given ground track situation.

Have students save or turn in their student sheets with graphs attached for use in Activity 5.

May the Force Be with You. Hand out Student Sheet 4.5 and grid paper, rulers, circular protractors, and calculators if they don't already have them. Explain that pilots frequently determine the effect of the wind by plotting scale drawings of vectors representing flight situations. Ask what this might entail. Groups are now going to simulate a pilot preparing for a flight. After plotting the appropriate vectors, students may choose to complete the wind parallelogram or use vector addition of the terminal coordinates to determine the ground-track vector.

While they are working, ask groups why there might be some variation in their conclusions. Entertain ideas relating to the uncertainty in measurement and the number of different measurements being made. During the subsequent class discussion concerning the effect wind has on the direction and speed of an airplane, examine their comprehension of vectors as well as their ability to determine ground track and ground speed.

Plane Techniques. Distribute Student Sheet 4.6, laminated state maps, spray bottles, sponges, transparency pens, circular protractors, yardsticks, calculators, and grid paper.

Explain to students they will work in pairs to choose reasonable data to represent a flight scenario and current wind information. Then they will chart the ground track and determine the ground speed for their particular flight. When they are finished, discuss the location of each plane after the elapsed flight time and its proximity to the intended destination. Ask, "What else does a pilot need to know in all of these situations?" After they conclude that a pilot ought to know how to alter the heading in the wind in order to stay on the true course and reach the intended destination, tell them the next activity addresses this issue.

Have students save or turn in to you the student sheets and graphs for use in Activity 5. Use the Technology Link "Wind Shear" and the Interest Link "Weather Conditions" at any time during the activity to spark student interest.

Discussion Questions

1. If an airplane's course vector is represented by the coordinates (11, 2) and the wind vector is represented by the coordinates (⁻5, 3), give the vector coordinates of the ground track.

   a. If the course vector is defined by (⁻5, 3) and the wind vector by (11, 2), how does this effect the vector defining the ground track? Explain your reasoning.

   b. Could either of these represent a realistic situation?

2. How is the speed of the wind related to the distance off course an airplane will be after one hour? After two hours?

3. If two vectors have the same direction and speed, they are considered equal vectors. What do equal vectors represent to the pilot or navigator?

Assessment Questions

1. A plane flying 155 mph is on a true-course heading of 080°. There is a wind blowing from 220° at 40 mph. Use vectors to determine the coordinates of the terminal point of the ground track after two hours in this wind.

2. Create your own set of coordinates to represent the terminal points of a true-course vector and a wind vector. Based on your data, predict the terminal coordinates for the ground track and verify your hypothesis. Give the wind forecast.

3. A plane is flying on a true course of 040° at 150 mph. During the first hour, a wind blows from 200° at 35 mph. During the second hour, the wind blows from 160° at 40 mph. Use vectors to plot the location of this plane after two hours.

Wind Shear

In 1985, a Delta jumbo jet made its landing approach to the Dallas-Fort Worth International Airport. Just before reaching the runway, however, the jet suddenly slammed into the ground, killing 134 of the 163 people on board. The cause of the tragic crash—wind shear. Wind shear has caused an estimated 26 aircraft accidents since 1964.

Wind shear is a violent, unpredictable change in wind direction. It occurs mostly at low altitudes. One form of wind shear, called a *microburst,* is a downdraft of wind that pours from the base of a cloud and spreads out horizontally. One scientist compares it to tap water hitting the bottom of a sink.

You can imagine how difficult it would be to pilot an airplane through wind shear. In the past decade, the government has ordered airports and airplanes to install wind-shear detection devices. But detecting wind shear is a difficult task. Detection devices sometimes cannot tell the difference between a downblast of wind and other phenomena, such as rain and even insects.

Wind-shear detectors continue to improve, however. Aviation researchers predict that in the near future, every plane will be equipped with a detector that warns pilots of wind shear. Pilots can successfully fly through wind shears, if they are warned in advance so they know how to maneuver the plane.

Weather Conditions

A pilot is required to determine that the existing and forecast weather conditions are suitable for flight. The weather information during the morning news on national network television gives a broad overview of national weather, but the best televised source of aviation weather is AM WEATHER, broadcast early in the morning on public television. This program, designed specifically for pilots, includes information on turbulence, winds aloft, icing, tops of buildups, location of pressure systems, and fronts.

To understand and anticipate weather changes, pilots must be aware of pressure systems and their movements. Cold air aloft is associated with low pressure and warm air aloft with high pressure. Air rising in a low pressure area draws air from outside the low into the center, and the general circulation pattern is counterclockwise. Air descending in a high pressure system circulates clockwise, and as the air reaches the surface it travels away from the center. Pilots on cross-country flights can take advantage of these circulation patterns to get favorable winds.

The dashed line represents a flight path from San Francisco to New Orleans that would take advantage of pressure systems.

A weather front exists where air masses with different properties meet. Cold air is more dense than warm air, so where two dissimilar masses meet, the cold air stays near the surface. When a cold front is advancing, it moves rapidly across the surface, forcing the warm air to rise in a narrow, vertical band. When a warm front overtakes a cold air mass, the warm air again rises, but continues its forward movement, as well. While cold fronts exist over a very short distance and provide a bumpy ride with potential showers, warm fronts can slope upward for many miles and allow for a smooth, rainy flight. A pilot can encounter hazardous structural icing if he flies into an area of freezing rain. It takes both visible moisture and temperatures below freezing to produce ice on an airplane. Either condition alone is comfortable for flying, but a pilot never wants to mix the two.

Where the Wind Blows

Wind direction is always reported as the direction from which the wind is blowing. A pilot immediately translates this information into the direction toward which the wind is blowing, which is the direction the wind is blowing the plane.

1. The wind forecast is for a 160° wind. This means the wind is blowing from 160° and is therefore, blowing the plane toward 340°. Draw a picture to illustrate this situation, and explain it in words.

2. For each situation below, the wind is blowing from the given direction. Determine toward what direction the wind is blowing the plane.

Wind Direction

From	Toward	From	Toward
120°		210°	
040°		255°	
090°		290°	
060°		330°	

3. If you know the direction from which the wind is blowing, how can you calculate the direction toward which it is blowing the plane? Explain your reasoning.

Parallelogram Plots

1. Use tractor strips or Polystrips™ to construct a wind parallelogram that represents an airplane flying 130 mph on a true course of 090° with a 40-mph wind blowing from 180°. Which direction is the wind blowing the plane? Explain your reasoning.

2. Use a full sheet of grid paper to prepare a set of coordinate axes that indicate the directions north, south, west, and east. Let one unit on the wind parallelogram equal 10 miles.

   a. Trace a copy of your wind parallelogram onto the paper, carefully aligning the starting point with the (0, 0) coordinate. Label the true-course and wind arrows.

   b. Determine and label the coordinates of the terminal point (endpoint) of the true-course arrow.

   c. Determine and label the coordinates of the terminal point (endpoint) of the wind arrow.

   d. List several things you know about the ground track of this flight.

Parallelogram Plots

3. Research the term *vector* and discuss with your group why the true-course and wind arrows are called vectors. Write your hypothesis below and be prepared to explain it to the class.

4. Is the ground track a vector? Explain your reasoning.

Vector Ventures

1. Prepare a set of coordinate axes on grid paper with direction arrows indicating north, south, west, and east. Let one unit on the grid paper equal 10 miles.

   a. For our purposes, we are going to assume all vectors originate at (0, 0).

   b. On your graph, draw the true-course vector that has terminal coordinates (14, 3). Label both the vector and its coordinates.

   c. Draw the wind vector that has terminal coordinates (2, 4). Again, label both the vector and its coordinates.

   d. Complete the resulting wind parallelogram.

   e. Draw the ground-track vector, determine its terminal coordinates, and label both the vector and its coordinates.

2. Describe your process for completing the wind parallelogram.

3. Determine the components of the true-course vector. Explain your reasoning.

4. Determine the components of the wind vector. Explain your reasoning.

5. Determine the components of the ground-track vector. Explain your calculations.

6. What does the ground-track vector represent in your drawings? Explain your reasoning.

Sum Vectors

1. For each situation below, prepare a separate set of coordinate axes on grid paper with direction arrows indicating north, south, west, and east.

   a. Use the given terminal coordinates to draw the true-course and the wind vector that originate at (0, 0). Label the vectors and coordinates.

   b. Complete the resulting wind parallelogram.

   c. Draw the ground-track vector and determine its terminal coordinates.

	Terminal Coordinates		
Situation	True-Course Vector	Wind Vector	Ground-Track Vector
i	(12, 4)	(2, 3)	
ii	(11, 2)	(‾5, 3)	
iii	(9, ‾8)	(‾1, 4)	
iv	(‾6, ‾13)	(‾2, 4)	

2. Describe how the coordinates of the ground-track vector are related to the coordinates of the wind vector and the true-course vector.

3. The coordinates for the terminal point of a ground-track vector with its initial point at (0, 0) are (12, 7). Plot this and determine the coordinates for the terminal points of the true course and the wind with this ground track. Explain your reasoning.

STUDENT SHEET 4.5

May the Force Be with You

Set up the following flight situations on grid paper and use vectors to determine the location of the plane. Let one unit on the grid paper equal 10 miles.

1. A pilot is flying on a true course of 040° at a speed of 130 mph. A wind is blowing from 160° at a speed of 30 mph.

   a. This airplane is tracking on a course of _____.

   b. The drift angle is _____.

   c. Is the wind increasing or decreasing the ground speed of the plane? Explain your reasoning.

   d. The ground speed of the plane is _____. Explain your process.

   e. After one hour, this plane is _____ miles off course.

   f. After two hours, this plane is _____ miles off course. Explain and illustrate your reasoning.

2. Another pilot is departing from a different airport on a 040° course at a speed of 130 mph. Now the wind is blowing from 010° with a speed of 50 mph.

   a. This airplane is tracking on a course of _____.

   b. The drift angle is _____.

May the Force Be with You

c. Is the wind increasing or decreasing the ground speed of the plane?
Explain your reasoning.

d. The ground speed of the plane is _____. Explain your process.

e. After one hour, this plane is _____ miles off course.

f. After two hours, this plane is _____ miles off course.

g. Would a pilot fly in this wind? Explain your reasoning.

Plane Techniques

For the following problem, plot a course line on the state map between two distant airports. With your partner, determine the compass heading and choose reasonable values to represent the speed of the plane as well as the direction and force of the wind. Complete the flight data in the table below.

1. A pilot is departing from _____ for _____ on a
                         (location)   (destination)
   true course of _____ degrees and flying at a speed of _____ mph.
   A northwest wind blowing from _____ degrees is blowing toward
   _____ degrees at a speed of _____ mph.

   a. Calculate the flight time in still air, and record this information in the flight data table.

Initial Flight Data

True Course	Airspeed	Distance	Flight Time

   b. Set up the situation on grid paper with one unit equals 10 mph and determine the ground track, drift angle, and ground speed based on the wind conditions.

Revised Flight Data

Wind From	Wind Toward	Wind Speed	Ground Track	Drift Angle	Ground Speed

   c. Based on the revised flight data, chart the plane's actual position after the elapsed flight time. Describe the geographical location of the plane.

   d. How far is this plane from its intended destination? Explain your process.

ACTIVITY
5

BACK ON TRACK

Overview

Students revisit several previous flight situations to determine the true heading a pilot must follow to compensate for prevailing winds. They explore a parallelogram method using tractor-feed strips or Polystrips™ and then a technique using vectors to identify the true heading and to calculate the adjusted ground speed. Students apply wind conditions to each leg of their original 1,000-mile journeys and complete detailed flight plans. The total time for their journeys are reassessed and compared to their original flight expectations from Activity 1, in which wind was not taken into account.

Time. Three or four 40- to 50-minute periods.

Purpose. Students learn that the *true heading,* the path a pilot must follow in order to arrive at the intended destination, usually differs from the direction of the true-course line. They gain understanding in the use of vectors for establishing a true heading and an adjusted ground speed in order to have the plane's flight path coincide with the true-course line. They also learn how a pilot calculates the actual flight time based on the true heading.

Materials. *For each student:*

◆ Student Sheets 5.1–5.5

◆ Completed Student Sheets 1.3, 3.3, 4.4, and 4.6.

◆ Ruler

◆ Circular protractor

◆ Grid paper

◆ Writing Link: Winds Aloft

For each pair of students:

◆ Tractor-feed strips from used computer paper or Polystrips™

◆ 8 brads

◆ Highlighter pen

◆ Calculator

◆ Construction compass

For the teacher:

◆ Transparencies of Student Sheets 5.1–5.5 (optional)

◆ Transparency Master 5.6

Getting Ready

1. Locate rulers, circular protractors, grid paper, tractor-feed strips or Polystrips™, brads, highlighters, calculators, and compasses.

2. Locate completed Students Sheets 1.3, 3.3, 4.4, and 4.6.

3. Duplicate Student Sheets 5.1–5.5 and the Writing Link Winds Aloft.

4. Prepare transparencies of Student Sheets 5.1–5.5 (optional).

5. Prepare Transparency Master 5.6.

Background Information

It is one thing to plot a course for flying in still air, a rare occurrence, and quite another to figure a course when the wind is blowing. Obviously, the force of the wind must be taken into account, in addition to the speed of the plane. The direction in which the wind is blowing is also of great importance, as the wind may either help or hinder the plane's progress.

By anticipating the amount of drift, pilots can counteract the effect of the wind, thereby making the ground track of the plane coincide with the desired course. They make corrections by turning the plane sufficiently into the wind to offset the drift angle. This becomes the *true heading,* defined as the direction the nose of the plane is pointing. The wind-correction angle is the difference between the true course and the true heading.

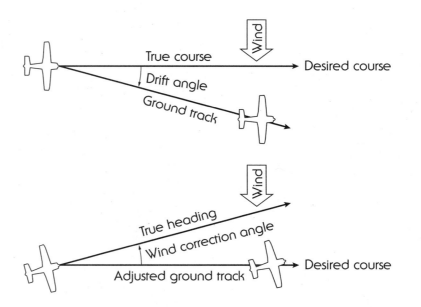

Calculating the wind-correction angle to determine the true heading involves trigonometry. Students may accurately estimate the true heading and the adjusted ground speed using geometric representations.

As pilots maintain their airspeed and alter the plane's heading into the wind, the resulting ground track and ground speed change based on the properties of a parallelogram.

The true course and airspeed along with the wind direction and speed actually provide enough information for two wind parallelograms. The first represents the anticipated flight plans, with the desired true-course vector and the wind vector. The parallelogram *WIND* below illustrates this. Note that the ground track does not coincide with the true course. The wind is pushing the plane off track.

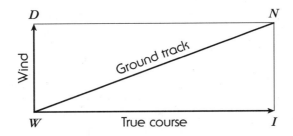

Pilots, using this same information, can also determine the correction needed to get the plane back on track. The wind, and therefore the wind vector *WD*, remains the same. Pilots have no control over the direction and speed of the wind. Their only recourse is to alter the course direction. Note that in the example above, the true course is 090° and the wind is from 180°. The wind is pushing the plane to the north. In order to get the plane back on track, the pilot needs to compensate for the wind by actually heading the plane into the wind, in a southerly direction. How far south to turn the plane is the question.

Recall that the ground track is always the diagonal of the wind parallelogram, so in order to have the ground track coincide with the true course, the desired course must become the diagonal of a second wind parallelogram, coinciding with *WI*.

Keeping the wind vector in exactly the same position, the pilot forms a second wind parallelogram by adjusting the direction of the course vector until *DN* intersects the original true-course vector at *N'*. The resulting ground track, *WN'*, called the *adjusted ground track*, now coincides with the true course, *WI*. *WI'*, called the *true heading*, gives the direction in which the plane must head in order to compensate for the prevailing wind.

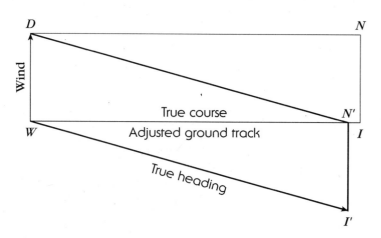

Note the adjusted ground track coincides with the true course, but since the lengths differ, it is not equal to it. The pilot, in order to compensate for the wind, heads the plane into the wind, and therefore, the adjusted ground speed, given by the length of the adjusted ground-track vector, will actually be less than the airspeed in this situation.

In the example pictured, the true course is 090° with airspeed equal to 150 mph. The wind is 40 mph from 180°. The true heading is approximately 105°, and the adjusted ground speed measures about 142 mph. Student Sheets 5.1 and 5.2 give students experience using wind parallelograms to determine the true heading and the adjusted ground speed.

Pilots can also use vectors to determine the true heading and adjusted ground speed. Using the same scale of 1 unit equals 10 mph, the above example is represented in terms of vectors, with their coordinates given. A pilot would use a construction compass to determine the length of the true-course vector. To determine the coordinates for the adjusted ground track, she would draw an arc with a span equal in length to the true-course vector, using the terminal point of the wind vector (0, 4) as the center of the arc. The arc would pass through the terminal point of the ground-track vector (15, 4), and the coordinates of the point where it intersects the true-course vector (or an extension of it) gives the terminal point of the adjusted ground track, (14.2, 0) in the example.

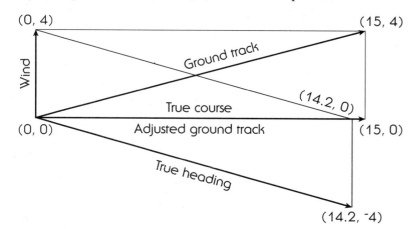

Once pilots know the coordinates of the terminal point of the adjusted ground track, they can use the scale of 1 unit equals 10 miles to mentally calculate the adjusted ground speed, which is 142 mph for the given example.

Establishing the coordinates for the terminal point of the adjusted ground track also allows pilots to locate the terminal coordinates for the true heading using vector subtraction. Let:

$\overrightarrow{WN}$ = Ground-Track Vector

$\overrightarrow{WI}$ = True-Course Vector

$\overrightarrow{WD}$ = Wind Vector

$\overrightarrow{WN'}$ = Adjusted Ground-Track Vector

$\overrightarrow{WI'}$ = True-Heading Vector

Since $\quad \overrightarrow{WN} = \overrightarrow{WI} + \overrightarrow{WD} \quad (15, 4) = (15, 0) + (0, 4)$

Then $\quad \overrightarrow{WN} - \overrightarrow{WD} = \overrightarrow{WI} \quad (15, 4) - (0, 4) = (15, 0)$

Similarly $\overrightarrow{WN'} - \overrightarrow{WD} = \overrightarrow{WI'} \quad (14.2, 0) - (0, 4) = (14.2, ^-4)$

Once pilots know the terminal point of the true heading, they can draw the vector and determine its orientation, which gives the direction they must head the plane in order to remain on the desired course.

On Student Sheet 5.3, students use vectors to determine the true heading and adjusted ground speed. On Student Sheet 5.4, students use either wind parallelograms, vectors, or both to determine true headings and adjusted ground speeds.

Pilots can plot and determine the true-course directions for a cross-country flight at any time prior to the journey, but the true headings are determined at the time of takeoff and periodically during flight as wind conditions change. If winds remain calm, the plane's track over the ground would be the same as the intended course and the ground speed would be the same as the true airspeed. Realistically, this is rarely the case. In actuality, pilots often take the wind conditions into account before determining their routes. Because of the prevailing wind, the fastest flight time may not correspond to the shortest route.

In Activity 1, students planned their 1,000-mile journeys assuming no wind except for a tail wind on leg two and a head wind on leg four. On Student Sheet 5.5, students complete actual flight plans for their 1,000-mile journeys that include true headings and adjusted ground speeds based on the actual forecast wind conditions for their state for that day. Reassessing their flight times will allow for two comparisons. They will note if these particular wind conditions increase or decrease their own flight times for the journey, as well as how the winds affect the class times and the winning routes.

Charting and interpreting wind parallelograms is a fundamental technique all pilots understand. Few of them actually draw wind parallelograms for determining the true heading and their adjusted ground speed, instead they use a special calculating device for this purpose. They must know, however, the fundamentals of wind parallelograms to know if their calculations are reasonable, as well as to have a backup in case the device does not work!

Use the Writing Link "Winds Aloft" and the Interest Link "Learning to Fly" at any time during the activity to enhance student interest.

Presenting the Activity

True Heading. Divide students into small working groups. Four to a group works well for this activity. Students can work in pairs and have discussions as a foursome.

Hand out or have students locate completed Student Sheet 3.3. Allow time for the groups to review the concepts and procedures involved in preparing a wind parallelogram. Elicit from the students what they think a pilot might need to do to get back on course when they know the wind is blowing them off their intended course. Ask if anyone has any ideas how a pilot might use a wind parallelogram to help them get back on course, or how a pilot can determine the true heading—the compass direction in which to point the nose of the plane in order to stay on the true course. Allow time for groups to discuss these ideas.

Distribute Student Sheet 5.1 and instruct students to work on the first three questions. As students complete their discussion on these questions, conduct a class discussion to summarize the ideas. Be sure they mention and agree on three possibilities for when the true heading is the same as the true course: when there is no wind, when the wind is a head wind, or when it is a tail wind. At all other times, the true course and the true heading differ. Ask them what effect each of these situations has on the ground speed of the plane. They may recall that the ground speed can range from the airspeed minus the wind speed to the air speed plus the wind speed.

Hand out tractor strips or Polystrips™, brads, circular protractors, calculators, highlighters, and rulers. Explain that the remaining work on this activity will help them discover how to use a wind parallelogram to calculate the true heading and the ground speed for a flight once the wind conditions are known.

As you circulate among groups, make sure they accurately align the brads of the constructed wind parallelogram with the true-course and wind vectors on their drawn wind vectors from question 1 on Student Sheet 3.3. Working in pairs, one student should hold the wind vector in place while the other student shifts only the course vector until the diagonal of the constructed wind parallelogram corresponds to the true-course vector of the original wind parallelogram. By marking several points, the pair can draw their second wind parallelogram in a different color to make it visually distinct from the original wind parallelogram.

Their measurement for the true heading will be approximately 198°, and the length of the ground-track vector gives an adjusted ground speed of approximately 125 mph.

When students are finished, use Transparency Master 5.6 to discuss the process of finding the second wind parallelogram that provides the true heading and adjusted ground speed. Discuss how to determine the ground speed, emphasizing that it is the length of the diagonal of the second wind parallelogram. Students should notice that even though the diagonal lies on the true course, it is not equal to it. Ask students why this happens.

Some may suggest the wind-correction angle, which lies between the true course and the true heading, is the same measure as the drift angle, though in the opposite direction. Accept this as a hypothesis, and explain that the next student sheet will provide more data.

Wind Correction. Hand out Student Sheet 5.2. Students also need their wind parallelograms, rulers, calculators, highlighters, circular protractors, and completed Student Sheet 3.3.

As students work in pairs to prepare each situation, listen to their discussions and watch their procedures. When you see situations where the wind increases the speed of the plane, suggest they extend the length of the true-course vector to find where the adjusted ground track intersects the true course.

In the summary discussion, some students may still believe the drift angle and wind-correction angle are equivalent measures. Though this can appear to be true, it is not. Remind them how 1° or 2° off course can affect an airplane's location, and explain that using trigonometry can provide an even more accurate reading.

Diagonals and Differences. Hand out or have students locate completed Student Sheet 4.4. Ask the class to review in groups how they derive terminal coordinates of the ground-track vector from knowing the terminal coordinates of the true-course and the wind vectors. Let them ponder how they might use this information to locate the terminal coordinates for the vector representing the true heading. Then hand out Student Sheet 5.3, construction compasses, rulers, and highlighters.

As students work in pairs, point out, if necessary, that they may need to extend the true-course vector in order to locate the adjusted ground-track vector for wind conditions that are increasing the speed of the plane. Again, suggest they draw the second parallelogram containing the true heading in a different color. For inclusion in follow-up discussions, note the different procedures students use for completing the wind parallelogram to locate the true heading.

Because of the number of approximations necessary, students may not readily see the inherent vector relationship. Their understanding of how the course and wind vectors combine to give the coordinates for the ground-track vector should allow them to accept the related subtraction situation where the ground track minus the wind provides the true-heading vector. Encourage them to check their true-heading coordinates by using vector addition to verify that the true heading plus the wind equals the adjusted ground-track vector.

Track and True. Hand out Student Sheet 5.4 and three sheets of grid paper to each student along with circular protractors, rulers, and calculators. Hand out or have students locate Student Sheet 4.6. Students may use either wind parallelograms or vectors or both to determine the true heading and adjusted ground speed in the various flight situations.

Inform students that for question 2, they will use information from Student Sheet 4.6 to complete the flight plans. Suggest they plot their individual situations on grid paper to analyze them.

In preparation for Activity 5, elicit what students know about the prevailing wind conditions in their state. Discuss that the next activity is going to focus on what a pilot does to get back on track. Explain that they will be recharting their 1,000-mile trip across the state incorporating actual forecast wind conditions for that day. Have them read the Writing Link, Winds Aloft, and allow time for discussion to ensure everyone understands what they need to do in order to get the necessary data.

Hand out or have teams locate the 1,000-mile journey plan on Student Sheet 1.3. Ask students how wind conditions might affect the outcomes of their journeys. It should be clear that on any given day, wind conditions will alter flight times and the actual course headings a pilot follows. Remind students to collect the wind forecast either right before they go to bed that night or in the morning before they come to school.

As the Wind Blows. Have students in their groups compare the wind forecasts. There might be differences based on the time collected and the altitude requested. Orchestrate a class discussion on which data would be the best to use. Take into consideration not only the most recent data, but also which altitudes might yield the best flight paths for the day. The class needs to reach consensus, and everyone should use the same wind forecasts.

Distribute Student Sheet 5.5, circular protractors, rulers, grid paper, and calculators. Ask how many students think they will complete their journey faster based on these winds. Record their hypotheses and have students explain their reasoning. Tell them to document their procedures on grid paper.

As they finish, ask each team how the total time of their journey compares to their hypothesis and to their previous time. Determine the fastest team based on these wind conditions, and decide how well that team's journey had fared in the original conditions. How well did the previous winning pair's journey perform in this weather? If you are flying in a cross-country race, when should you plan your route?

Discussion Questions

1. How and when can a pilot decide if the adjusted ground speed will be faster or slower than the airspeed?

2. The weather report from Seattle, Washington, indicates there is a 30-mph northwest wind in effect.

   a. Will each pilot departing from Seattle use the same wind correction angle? Explain your reasoning.

   b. Will every pilot departing from Seattle for Yakima, Washington, apply the same wind correction angle? Explain your reasoning.

3. Why do planes take off and land into the wind?

4. What does mathematics have to do with navigation?

Assessment Questions

1. Chart two approximately 150-mile flights from your city to airports located in the east and the west of the state. Two planes are departing for these destinations at airspeeds of 150 mph. A 25-mph wind from 210° is forecast.

   a. Which plane will arrive at its destination first? Explain your reasoning.

   b. Determine the true heading, adjusted ground speed, and flight time for each plane.

c. If the pilot flying west sets the compass for the true course instead of the true heading, determine the plane's location after one hour. Decide what heading the pilot should follow from this point to arrive at the intended destination.

2. A Boeing 737 departs Sea-Tac (Seattle/Tacoma airport) at 9:00 A.M. for a 980-mile flight to LAX (Los Angeles airport) flying at a cruising altitude of 35,000 feet. The true course is 190° and the airspeed is approximately 500 mph. A 55-mph wind is blowing from 300°.

   a. What is the true heading the pilot will use and the adjusted ground speed?

   b. What is the estimated time of arrival?

   c. If the pilot makes a navigation error of 5°, how many miles off course will the plane be after 980 miles?

3. A plane traveling at an airspeed of 180 mph departed on a true course of 160°. Because of the wind, this plane is actually on a ground track of 152° and flying at a ground speed of 165 mph.

   a. Determine the direction and speed of the wind.

   b. Determine the true heading, adjusted ground track, and adjusted ground speed.

Winds Aloft

A pilot will always consult the local Flight Service Station of the National Weather Service for preflight weather briefing. Jeppesen/ Sanderson issues a Flight Plan map showing the location of every Flight Service Station in the United States. In Washington State, the toll-free number is 1-800-992-7433. A pilot can call and consult with a pre-flight briefer who inputs your flight plan into a computer and gives you the winds aloft conditions that are most appropriate for each leg of your flight at the altitude requested.

Winds aloft are issued twice daily in increments of 3000 feet. Conditions are reported from several locations within a state. There are three reporting locations in Washington State: Seattle, Yakima, and Spokane. In many places, this information is acquired by launching expensive weather balloons equipped with radio transmitters. This rather archaic method is slowly being replaced by Doppler radar readings and satellite pictures.

The winds aloft forecast is the first thing to check in choosing a cruising altitude for favorable winds. A Cessna 172 has a ceiling of 12,000 feet. Pilots look for rapid changes in wind direction or speed across altitude levels as a warning of turbulence. In general, the higher the elevation, the stronger the wind force. For example, a head wind at 9,000 feet may be at 34 mph, while at 6,000 feet, it's 23 mph, and at 3,000 feet it's 14 mph. In this situation, when the geography allows, a pilot will fly at 3,000 feet to conserve fuel and time. It's also possible for the winds aloft at 3,000 feet to be easterly, while at 6,000 feet they are westerly!

The wind speeds and directions that pilots use in flight planning are forecast winds. The National Weather Service wind direction forecasts are in 10° increments and can be off as much as 45° before a corrected forecast is issued, therefore, pilots must consider that the data is approximate. For a departure heading, pilots use the winds aloft forecast from the closest reporting station. In flight, pilots may need to adjust their ground track to compensate for changing wind conditions. Pilots radio flight watch stations enroute for immediate weather conditions or their local Flight Service Station to receive updated forecasts and assistance in adjusting their heading. In general, pilots adjust their true heading based on the proximity of reporting stations enroute. For example, in Washington State, a pilot flying from Olympia to Pasco calculates a departure heading using the winds aloft forecast from the Seattle reporting station, then adjusts the true heading based on the Yakima station winds aloft forecast as they cross the Cascade Mountains. If there is little variation in wind conditions from the reporting stations enroute, a pilot may average the forecasts and apply one heading for the entire journey.

Since many planes are equipped with wind sensors, pilots always call the local reporting station and provide existing wind conditions. Other pilots calling for winds aloft information are given these updates along with the current forecast. Stations rely on pilot updates, but the forecast is rarely revised, even when the existing conditions vary radically from the current forecast.

Call the Flight Service Station nearest to your home airport. Explain the trip you are planning, and collect the wind forecasts needed to prepare your flight plans. Write a brief report of your findings to present to the class.

Learning to Fly

Many pilots were still young when they first became interested in flying, perhaps after flying with a licensed pilot. To encourage young people's interest in flying, groups throughout the country offer programs in aviation. The programs range from orientation flights to aerospace education. One of several national organizations such as the American Institute for Aeronautics and Astronautics, the Civil Air Patrol, and the Experimental Aircraft Association may sponsor youth programs in your area.

As a teenager, you can begin taking flying lessons from a Federal Aviation Association (FAA) certified instructor or a flight training school at a local airport. Right from the beginning, you will do most of the actual flying. After the takeoff and climb-out by your instructor, you will take over. At first you will try to stay on a straight and level course. As lessons continue, you will make gentle turns, then progress to steeper turns. You'll find out what glides and climbs feel like and what stalls are all about. Following several lessons, you'll start making takeoffs and landings while you continue to practice other maneuvers.

At age 16, you can obtain a student pilot certificate, which allows you to fly an airplane alone. For a private certificate, you must be 17 years old with a minimum of 40 hours of flight time.

You can also learn to fly hot air balloons. Though balloons are simpler to operate than planes, FAA regulations require a balloon pilot to have a license. You can get a student license at 14 but must be 16 to be licensed to take passengers in your balloon. Most balloon rides are for recreation and pilots choose to fly in the early morning or evening when wind speeds are low. If a cross-country trip is planned in a balloon, it must be in the direction of the wind.

Another alternative is to build and fly remote control gliders. Operating gliders helps you understand the aerodynamic forces that influence flight. Flying remote planes will give you opportunities to apply flight techniques, to see how wind affects flight, and to learn to use wind to your advantage.

True Heading

Using a wind parallelogram, a pilot determines the true heading, which is the direction the pilot must fly to maintain the plane's desired course.

1. When is the true heading for a flight the same direction as the true course? Explain your reasoning and discuss it with your group.

2. When is the true heading for a flight a different direction than the true course? Explain your reasoning and discuss it with your group.

3. If an airplane is following a ground track that is north of the true course, what direction will the pilot head the plane in order to arrive at the intended destination? Explain your reasoning.

4. With your partner, build a wind parallelogram representing an airplane flying at an airspeed of 130 mph with a 40-mph wind.

5. Refer to your drawing from question 1 on Student Sheet 3.3. It represents a true course of 180° with the wind blowing 090° due east. Follow these steps to determine the true heading for this flight.

   a. Align your wind parallelogram with your original grid paper drawing.

   b. One person holds the wind vector strip in place while the other person shifts the parallelogram until the ground-track vector coincides with the true-course vector (or an extension of it) in your drawing.

   c. Accurately outline in a different color the second wind parallelogram onto your initial drawing.

True Heading

6. Where is the ground track located for the second wind parallelogram? Explain your reasoning and discuss it with your group. Label it the adjusted ground track (AGT) in your drawing.

7. Determine the true heading that allows the pilot to fly along the intended true course. Explain your process.

8. Determine the wind correction angle for this flight. Explain your procedures.

9. When the pilot is flying the true heading, is the plane traveling slower or faster than its airspeed? Explain your reasoning.

10. Determine the plane's adjusted ground speed. Explain your process.

Wind Correction

The true heading allows the adjusted ground track to coincide with the true course.

1. With your partner, rebuild a wind parallelogram representing an airplane flying at an airspeed of 130 mph with a 40-mph wind.

2. Refer to your drawings from question 4 on Student Sheet 3.3. Repeat steps 5 a–c given on Student Sheet 5.1 to determine the true heading for a plane flying 130 mph on an intended 180° course with a 40-mph wind. Clearly label your wind parallelograms, and record the data in the table given below.

3. Refer to your drawings from question 5 on Student Sheet 3.3. Repeat steps 5 a–c given on Student Sheet 5.1 to determine the true heading for a plane flying 130 mph on an intended 180° course with a 40-mph wind from another direction. Clearly label your wind parallelograms, and record the data in the table given below.

Question	True Course	Wind Direction	Drift Angle	True Heading	Correction Angle	Adjusted Ground Speed
2.						
3.						

4. Why does the wind parallelogram method work for determining the true heading?

Wind Correction

5. Is the adjusted ground-track vector equal to the true-course vector? Explain your reasoning.

6. Determine the wind-correction angle for both of your flights and record them in the above table.

7. When the pilot in question 2 is flying the true heading, is the plane traveling faster or slower than its airspeed? Explain your reasoning.

8. When the pilot in question 3 is flying the true heading, is the plane traveling faster or slower than its airspeed? Explain your reasoning.

9. Determine the adjusted ground speed for both of your flight situations and record the results in the table.

10. Another pilot flying 130 mph is in a 40-mph wind from 025° and on a true heading of 110°. Determine the true course for this flight. Explain your procedures.

Diagonals and Differences

1. With your partner, follow these steps to construct a second wind parallelogram that will give the coordinates for the true heading and the adjusted ground track for each vector display from Student Sheet 4.4.

   a. Open the compass span to the length of the true-course vector. Place the compass point on the terminal point of the wind vector and draw an arc that intersects the true-course vector or an extension of it.

   b. Determine and label the coordinates for this point of intersection that represents the terminal point for the adjusted ground track (AGT). Connect this point to the terminal point of the wind vector, creating a new vector. This new vector and the wind vector can then be used to create a second wind parallelogram that has as its diagonal the AGT vector.

   c. Complete the second wind parallelogram and outline it with a highlighter.

   d. Determine and label the coordinates of the terminal point for the true-heading vector. Record the data in the table.

Situation	Terminal Coordinates			
	Course Vector	Wind Vector	Adjusted Ground Track	True Heading
i	(12, 4)	(2, 3)		
ii	(11, 2)	(⁻5, 3)		
iii	(9, ⁻8)	(⁻1, 4)		
iv	(⁻6, ⁻13)	(⁻2, 4)		

Diagonals and Differences

2. In each situation, is the plane flying slower or faster than its airspeed? Explain your reasoning.

3. Describe how the coordinates of the true heading are related to the other coordinates.

Track and True

1. Plot the following navigational situations on grid paper. Determine the wind parallelogram for each problem. Locate the second wind parallelogram to determine the true heading in order to maintain the desired course. Then calculate the adjusted ground speed (AGS). Record the information in the table provided. Let one unit equal 10 miles.

   a. Situation A: A plane is flying on a true course of 080° at a speed of 165 mph. The wind is blowing from 130° at a speed of 40 mph.

True Course	Airspeed	Wind From	Wind Toward	Wind Speed	Correction Angle	True Heading	AGS

   b. Situation B: Another plane is departing on a true course of 230° at a speed of 140 mph. The wind is blowing from 350° at a speed of 35 mph.

True Course	Airspeed	Wind From	Wind Toward	Wind Speed	Correction Angle	True Heading	AGS

2. Refer to question 1 on Student Sheet 4.6. Complete the flight plan by determining the true heading the pilot will fly in order to arrive at the intended destination. Determine the adjusted ground speed as well. Record the information below.

True Course	Airspeed	Wind From	Wind Toward	Wind Speed	Correction Angle	True Heading	AGS	Distance

3. Based on the adjusted ground speed above, calculate the revised flight time for your journey.

As the Wind Blows

With your partner, complete the first four columns of the Wind Chart by referring to Student Sheet 1.3. Fill in the wind forecast information for each leg of the flight for the forecast station closest to your take-off point, and also for the forecast station nearest your destination point. With your partner, decide when and if you will change from one station to the next. Use grid paper to accurately calculate necessary information to file a completed flight plan. Combine this chart with the flight plan for a complete picture of your 1,000 mile journey.

Wind Chart

Leg	Location	Destination	True Course	Air Speed	Wind From	Wind Toward	Wind Speed	Wind Change Location
1.								
2.								
3.								
4.								
5.								
6.								

As the Wind Blows

Flight Plan

Depart Time	True Heading	Adjusted Ground Speed	Distance	Fuel*	Usage	Flight Time	Arrival Time
1. 9:00 A.M.							
2.							
3.							
4.							
5.							
6.							

* Indicates a stop for refueling   Total [ ]   Total [ ]

Average ground speed for the journey is _____.

Total time including stopovers is _____.

Did your lunch plans change?

Back on Track

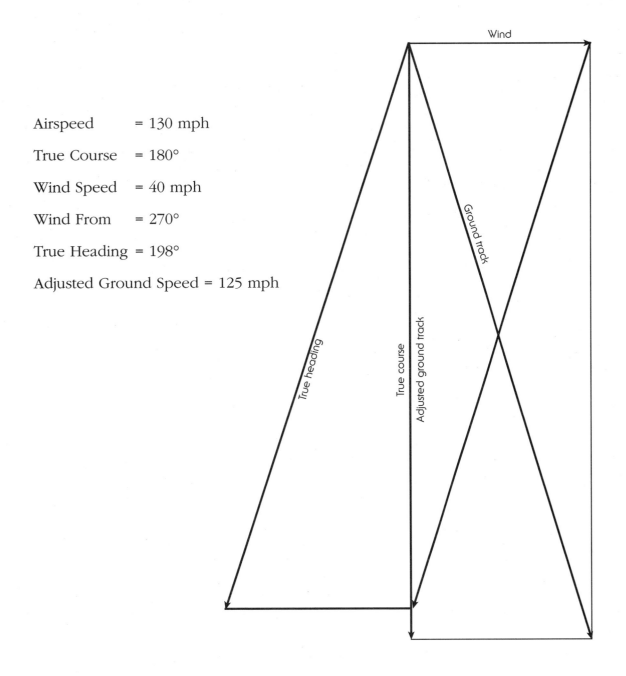

Airspeed   = 130 mph

True Course   = 180°

Wind Speed   = 40 mph

Wind From   = 270°

True Heading = 198°

Adjusted Ground Speed = 125 mph

WIND TUNNEL

Overview

Students and their families are introduced to the forces involved in flight—lift, drag, weight, and thrust. They conduct several experiments that illustrate Bernoulli's principle, the scientific basis behind aircraft design. Families build simple wind tunnels in which they test the aerodynamics of various objects, enabling them to understand aspects of the career of an aeronautical engineer.

Time. Approximately three hours following Activity 5.

Purpose. With their families, students discover why things fly. They develop a comprehension of how properties of air contribute to flight and what design features enhance the aerodynamics of an object. They appreciate the problem-solving basis of a career in aeronautics.

Materials. *For each family group:*
◆ Family Activity Sheets 1–4
◆ Notebook paper
◆ Scissors
◆ Paper clips
◆ 2 large, identical cardboard boxes
◆ Electric fan
◆ 4–8 sets of identical box inserts used to separate glass bottles
◆ 1 small utility hook
◆ Transparency
◆ Masking tape
◆ Lightweight string
◆ Tape measure or ruler
◆ Knife
◆ Objects for flight testing (see Family Activity Sheet 3)

For the teacher:
◆ Transparency of Family Activity 2

Getting Ready

1. Duplicate Family Activity Sheets 1–4.
2. Locate a transparency sheet for each family.
3. Prepare transparency.

Background Information

In this activity, students and their families expand their understanding of how wind affects aircraft. After completing a few elementary experiments to clarify Bernoulli's principle, each family builds a simple wind tunnel to use for testing and analyzing the aerodynamic properties of various objects.

Aerodynamics is the science that deals with air moving against an object, such as an airplane flying through the sky. Four forces are at work when an airplane is flying. They are thrust, drag, lift, and weight. Thrust moves it forward. Drag holds it back. When thrust and drag are equal, the plane continues to move at its intended speed. Lift pushes it up. Weight pulls it down. When lift and weight are equal, the plane remains at the same altitude, without climbing higher or dropping lower.

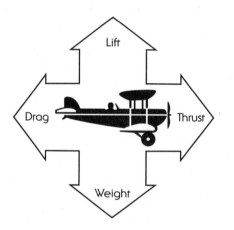

The top surface of an airplane's wing is curved while the bottom surface is flat. This shape is called an *airfoil*. As the plane cuts through the air, the air flowing over the top of the wing has to travel a greater distance than the air flowing underneath the wing, therefore the air travels faster over the top. It is a scientific principle, called Bernoulli's principle, that air pressure decreases when the flow of air speeds up. Because there is less pressure on the top surface of an airplane's wing than on the bottom, the wing is pushed upward. This upward force is called *lift*, and the lift is greater the faster the airplane travels.

Simply stated, an airplane flies because the pilot causes it to accelerate down the runway until the wings develop a lifting force greater than the plane's weight. A plane lands because the pilot causes the lifting force to be less than the plane's weight.

The plane is held back by drag. The faster an airplane flies, the more drag occurs. Drag is a particular problem in designing high-speed planes because drag increases much faster than the speed of the plane. The larger an airplane's wings are, the more it can lift; but the larger they are, the more drag they have, too. With the same amount of thrust, an airplane with larger wings can lift more weight than an airplane with smaller wings, but it cannot fly as fast.

Angles or sharp curves on objects break up the airflow and cause eddies, or swirls of air, increasing drag. Planes, cars, and trains are all designed with smooth, curved bodies to reduce drag. All parts of the plane that are in contact with the air are streamlined. Streamlining helps the air flow smoothly over the plane. A car with a streamlined shape will go faster and use less fuel because it has low drag. Modern trucks have specially designed cab roofs that direct the airflow up and over the load behind them.

Aeronautical engineers test models of planes in wind tunnels, which blow an air stream over the models. Air streams from wind-tunnel fans can move up to 20 times the speed of sound. If smoke is put into the tunnel, the designers can see how the air flows around the model. By making adjustments, they can find the most efficient aerodynamic shape. Students with their families can read more about wind tunnels in the Technology Link "Wind Tunnels."

Presenting the Activity

Divide the class into groups of three or four students. Use the top graphic on Family Activity Sheet 2 to present the four forces acting upon an object in flight. Acknowledge that these four forces work on paper planes as well as real planes.

Thrust is any force that pushes or pulls an airplane forward through air. In a discussion, have students present various forms of thrust. These may include the human hand that throws a paper plane, a rubber band that launches a model, the action of a propeller, or a jet engine. Ask them if thrust alone is enough to make an airplane fly. They may respond by noting that cars and trains, no matter how fast they go, cannot fly.

Define *drag* as the force that comes from the resistance of the air, which slows down any moving object. Have groups give examples of when they have experienced the effects of drag. These may come from biking, skiing, water sports, or simply walking against the wind. Then ask how they might reduce the drag in each scenario. Students may consider the notion of streamlining.

In addition to thrust, flight requires an uplifting force. Elicit ideas on what provides lift—the force that allows an aircraft to move in three dimensions. Students may have a sense that wing design and streamlining features contribute to moving an airplane upward, but may not be clear on how or why this happens.

Suggest they each tear a 2-inch strip from a sheet of notebook paper. Have them hold the strips against their lower lips as they gently blow over the upper surface as outlined in question 1 on Family Activity Sheet 1. Have groups describe the results and hypothesize why the lift occurs. Explain that this activity demonstrates the Bernoulli principle, which says moving air has a lower pressure than the air around it. Since the air pressure below the strip of paper is heavier, the strip rises.

Use the lower graphic on Family Activity 2 to illustrate how this theory is applied in designing a wing that promotes lift. Because of curvature, air travels a longer distance on the upper portion of the wing. The airspeed over the wing increases in order for the air to arrive at the end of the wing at exactly the same time as the air moving under the wing. As a result, the air pressure is less on the upper portion. This causes the lift.

Weight, or gravity, is the force constantly pulling an airplane toward the ground. If an airplane is to stay in the air, the forces of thrust and lift must be stronger than those of drag and weight. Paper airplanes eventually succumb to gravity.

Distribute the family activity sheets. Explain the project and clarify your expectations. The three-hour suggested time for this activity is approximate; the time required will vary from family to family. Give students a reasonable time period, perhaps spanning a weekend, to complete Family Activity Sheet 3. They will need this to arrange adequate family time to find the materials and to work on the project. Schedule two separate due dates in order to discuss Family Activities 1–3 in class prior to the start of the wind-tunnel tests. Explain that on the day the activities are due, each student will give a short presentation to describe the experience and results.

What Makes an Airplane Fly? On the day after students complete Family Activity Sheets 1–3 with their families, divide the class into groups of three or four to compare results. Students should further understand that by blowing on the strip or running with it, the air velocity increases, which lowers the pressure on the upper surface. The pressure or velocity of the air under the paper has not been disturbed. The result is that the pressure under the paper is greater than the pressure on top, thereby providing a lifting action.

In addition to comprehending Bernoulli's principle, students should also recognize that it does not matter whether they blow on the strip or pull the strip through the air. This is one of the theories behind the use of a wind tunnel. Suspended models mimic the effects of wind on an airplane that is flying.

Collect data on how many paper clips students were able to lift. Ask them what might have caused the variation in numbers. They may list the force of the wind or airspeed in their remarks. Summarize the results as a class, and ask them how they might use these results to develop their wind-tunnel tests.

Making a Wind Tunnel and Wind-Tunnel Tests. Provide a few minutes of class time each day prior to the project due date for groups to briefly discuss how things are progressing with their wind-tunnel construction and testing. Any troubleshooting, modification suggestions, or ideas concerning objects to test may provide insights or generate further thought for other students.

On the day reports are due, have students discuss their data in groups, and then conduct a class discussion to summarize the trials and findings from each group.

Discussion Questions

1. Which objects flown in the wind tunnel seemed to have the least drag? How did you determine this?

2. Based on your experiments, why do planes take off and land into the wind?

3. What did your wind tunnel show you about streamlining?

4. What effect does the weight of an object have on its aerodynamics? Give actual test data to substantiate your reasoning.

5. Do the objects you are testing tend to move toward or away from the fan? Why?

Wind Tunnels

A wind tunnel is a chamber through which air is forced at controlled speeds to study the airflow around an object. Some wind tunnels are so large that huge planes fit inside them. But researchers often use smaller tunnels and suspend or mount models in them. Models cost less and may be modified more easily than the planes. Wind tunnels also allow researchers to simulate conditions that would be impossible or dangerous in flight.

Based on the fact that air moving past a stationary model creates the same force as if the model were flying through still air, wind tunnel experiments provide valid representations of what will actually happen in flight.

Although they were not the first to employ a wind tunnel, the Wright brothers built and used a wind tunnel before they made their first successful flight in 1903. A circular section directed the air flow through the box-shaped test section. A dual-bladed, 24-inch diameter fan, driven by a two-horsepower gasoline engine, produced a maximum speed of 27 mph.

The brothers experimented with models and learned about wing curves, lifting forces, air resistance, and efficient wing designs. They observed the laws of physics that aided or prevented flight, and then applied the helpful forces and overcame the inhibiting ones in their final design. A model of their original tunnel resides at Henry Ford's Greenfield Village in Dearborn, Michigan.

While the design of wind tunnels today has not undergone much change, the advancements in technology allow for more sophisticated analysis of the tests. The Illinois Institute of Technology recently built a wind tunnel using a 2,000-horsepower engine that blasts air at 550 mph. The tunnel is used to find ways to reduce drag on plane wings, trains, cars, and other vehicles.

NASA built the world's largest wind tunnel at the Ames Research Center in Mountain View, California. The tunnel is 80 feet by 120 feet and uses 135,000-horsepower motors to turn six fans. The Ames home page on the World-Wide Web often includes information on their wind tunnel. See what you can find. Try the address http://ccf.arc.nasa.gov/wind_tunnel/homepage.html.

Section of Wright Brothers' Wind Tunnel from the collection of the Henry Ford Museum and Greenfield Village.

Aeronautical Engineer

Have you ever folded a paper airplane? Did you experiment with the way you folded it to create an airplane that flew straight and fast as an arrow, or one that soared and looped? If so, you have done what aeronautical engineers do. They study aerodynamics and design flying machines.

Aerodynamics is the study of forces acting on objects—such as airplanes—due to air. It is closely linked to *aeronautics,* the study of flight.

Aeronautical engineers are interested in the way things fly. Some strive to design better planes that fly faster, use less fuel, or carry more passengers. Others create never-before-imagined flying machines—cars that fly, jets that can take off from rooftops, or military planes that are as silent as gliders. Still others test new aircraft or study noise pollution or, if they work in a branch of aeronautics called *aerospace technology,* develop spaceships. There are many roles for aeronautical engineers.

Aeronautical engineers work in manufacturing plants, at universities, in laboratories, and for a broad field of employers including the National Aeronautics and Space Administration (NASA) and airline companies.

Engineers need bachelor's degrees for most jobs, and many also have engineering licenses and advanced degrees as well. With all the advancements in technology, the future for engineering professionals is promising. Salaries range from $30,000 a year for starting job to an average of $50,000 a year with experience.

When human-powered flight began, it was a highly dangerous endeavor for the courageous. In less than a century, it has grown to one of the most complex, exacting, and advanced technologies known. An amazing array of equipment and accomplishments have followed those first flights, each new advance building on the foundation of previous research, development, and testing.

Aerospace and aeronautical engineering and technology is probably the most specialized and yet the most diversified field there is. Aerospace professionals apply their knowledge to build better planes, to send spacecraft to Mars, or to design satellites for predicting the weather. Yet these same engineers may also design an energy-efficient skyscraper, study how the wind affects a new building in a large urban area, or do research for an artificial heart.

What Makes an Airplane Fly?

1. Cut a 2-inch strip of notebook paper. Place one end of it against your lower lip. Gently blow along the upper surface of the strip. Describe what happens.

2. Try the above experiment after you have fastened a paper clip on the end of the strip. How many paper clips can you lift in this way?

3. Remove the paper clips. Hold the strip of paper in your hand and run around the room. What do you observe?

4. Based on the paper's behavior, does it matter whether you move the air over the paper or move the paper through the air? Explain your reasoning.

FAMILY ACTIVITY SHEET 1 (cont'd)

What Makes an Airplane Fly?

5. What do you think will happen to two sheets of notebook paper if you hold them about 4 inches apart and blow between them?

6. Try the above experiment and describe what actually happens. Did the results surprise you? Explain why you think this occurs.

7. One of the most significant discoveries that led to the creation of an airfoil is the Bernoulli principle. Daniel Bernoulli (1700–1782) developed a theory concerning the behavior of fluids. Because air is a fluid, his theory has been accepted as a partial explanation of how air pressure and velocity interact on an airfoil to provide the lift necessary for flight. Bernoulli's principle states that moving air has a lower pressure than the still air around it. If the air moves rapidly on one side of a surface, the pressure on that side is less than that on its other side. Explain how these activities illustrate this theory.

Four Forces in Flight

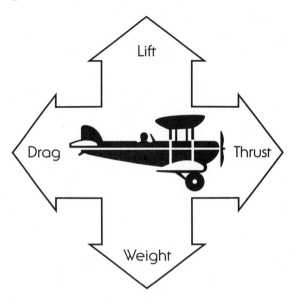

Discuss how these four forces influence the plane's movement through the air.

Air Flow

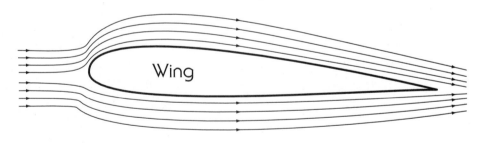

The air moving over the curved top of the wing has a greater distance to travel than the air moving under the wing. It must travel faster to arrive at the back of the wing at the same time as air traveling under the wing. Bernoulli's principle states that faster-moving air has less pressure. Discuss what happens to the wing.

Making a Wind Tunnel

Materials

- 2 large, identical cardboard boxes like those used for packaging paper towels, with the flaps still attached (can be obtained from a local grocery store in the late evening when they are stocking shelves)
- Electric fan that will fit inside the box, preferably with adjustable speeds
- 4–8 sets of identical inserts commonly used as separators in boxes to separate glass bottles.
- 1 small utility hook, the kind used for hanging cups
- Transparency for the window
- Masking tape
- Lightweight string
- Tape measure or ruler
- Knife

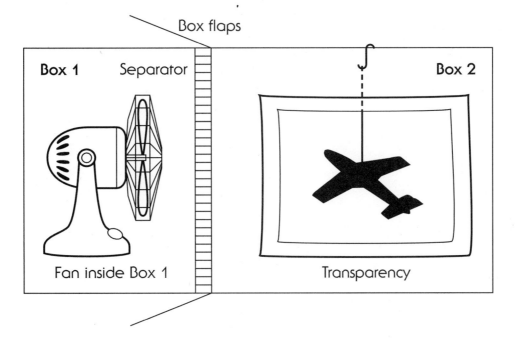

This wind tunnel design is by Bob Kelley-Wickemeyer, an aerodynamicist for the Boeing Company.

Making a Wind Tunnel

Instructions

Open both ends of the boxes. Based on the size of your fan, decide which side of the box will be the top of the wind tunnel. Push the flaps on one end of each box toward the inside for added strength.

Open the inserts and overlap them together so they will fit snugly as one unit in front of the fan in the first box. It may be necessary to cut off part of the inserts; then connect and reinforce them with tape, and secure the inserts in the box with tape. These separators act as a honeycomb to straighten the swirling air currents from the electric fan.

Without actually attaching them together, overlap the extended flaps to connect the boxes to form the wind tunnel. This allows you to easily disassemble the tunnel. Use a knife to cut an 8-by-10-inch window near the end of the second box. Cover the window with the transparency and secure it with tape. Fasten the hook in the box so when an object is suspended from it, you can see it through the window.

Set the electric fan inside the box containing the separators to complete the wind tunnel as shown.

Wind Tunnel Tests

"Model airplane builders in particular will be interested in seeing the performance of their models in an air stream, and some may find that their simple experiments lead to new discoveries in airplane design."
—Charles Ludington, author of *Smoke Streams*

1. Select various objects from the list below and any others of your own choosing to suspend in your wind tunnel.

   a small cube   single-serving cereal box   paper airplanes
   table tennis ball   half a lemon   model airplanes
   tennis ball   toy football
   hard-boiled egg   empty soup can

2. Tape one end of an approximately 18-inch piece of string onto an object. Make a loop in the other end of the string to suspend the object from the hook so it is visible in the center of the window. You may want to place string hangers in various positions on each object to observe the effects of the wind. On some items, you may want to attach the hanger at the point of balance. Some objects may need to be wrapped securely with string before they will hang.

3. Hypothesize what you think might happen before you test each object, then observe and describe the results when an air stream is present. Be sure to orient objects in more than one way and watch what happens.

4. If you have a fan with adjustable speeds, observe how a change in wind speed influences the aerodynamics of an object.

5. Research the meaning of *aerodynamics*. Discuss the term with your family and compose a definition of it.

Wind Tunnel Tests

6. Write a report on your wind tunnel experiments that includes how a wind tunnel demonstrates aerodynamic performance.

   a. Describe the aerodynamic characteristics of objects that fly well.

   b. Describe the aerodynamic problems of objects that do not fly well.

   c. According to your aerodynamic analysis, what specific aircraft design features are desirable? Which are not?

Extensions

7. Begin with a paper airplane design you have tested in your wind tunnel. Based on the testing, modify or redesign it to increase the aerodynamics. Record your modifications, procedures, and observations.

8. Design a testing situation to determine if and how weight influences aerodynamics. Describe your procedures and substantiate your conclusions.

9. Replace the second box in your wind tunnel construction with one that is similar to the first box, but about two-thirds the size of it. Conduct wind-tunnel tests to decide the effect of this alteration. Which tunnel design do you prefer? Explain your reasoning.

COMPLETED
STUDENT
SHEETS

Flight Paths

Flying involves knowing where you are, where you want to go, which way to go, and how fast you are going.

1. With your partner, choose an airport on the state map to begin your journey and mark its location with a point. Draw a direction arrow from your departure point that represents true north. Use the indicator for north on your map as a guide.

2. Select another airport in the state as your destination. Draw a course line connecting the two airports.

3. Measure the angle the course line makes with true north to determine your course heading and direction of flight.

4. Complete the flight plan for a Cessna 172 flying at an airspeed of 150 mph. Label the course line with the direction on top and the distance below.

	Departure Location	Destination	Course Heading	Distance	Flight Time
Initial Flight					
Return Flight	*Responses will vary*				

5. Are the initial flight and return flight directions the same? Why or why not? *No. The direction for a return flight on the same course line is the opposite direction from the initial flight. There will be a plus or a minus 180° difference.*

6. Are the initial flight and return flight distances the same? Why or why not? *Yes. If the same course line is followed, the distance between two points is constant.*

Navigation

Navigation means knowing where you are and how to determine a course to where you want to go.

1. Can someone correctly locate a friend's house if she knows it is one block from her house? Why or why not? *Not necessarily. She does not know if the house is one block east, west, north, or south.*

2. Can someone deliver a paper to the correct house if he knows it is east of his house? Why or why not? *Not necessarily. He does not know how far east to travel.*

3. Can someone return a tool to a neighbor if she knows he lives two blocks north of her house? Why or why not? *Maybe. She knows the direction and how far to go, but there may be more than one house at the point two blocks north.*

4. If you are giving someone directions, what kind of information should you include? *Include the compass direction in which to travel and the distance to go in that direction.*

Plane Tracks

3. Do the pen tracks on the bottom sheet of grid paper follow the 090° course line? Why or why not?
   No. The paper upon which the pen was moving east was simultaneously being pulled north.

4. Sketch the track marks with respect to the 10-unit, 090° true course line and the 10-unit wind arrow pointing 000° north. Explain what the pen tracks represent.

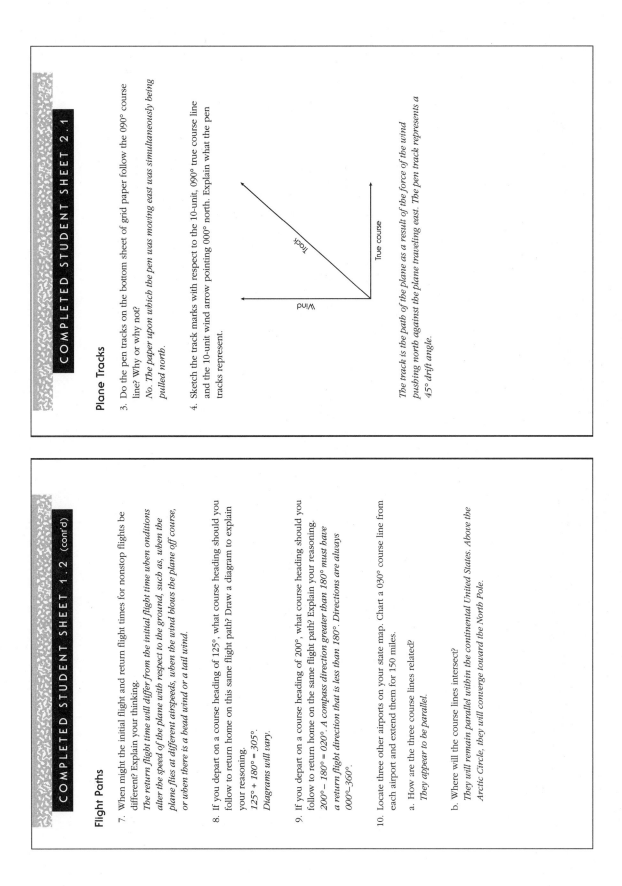

The track is the path of the plane as a result of the force of the wind pushing north against the plane traveling east. The pen track represents a 45° drift angle.

Flight Paths

7. When might the initial flight and return flight times for nonstop flights be different? Explain your thinking.
   The return flight time will differ from the initial flight time when onditions alter the speed of the plane with respect to the ground, such as, when the plane flies at different airspeeds, when the wind blows the plane off course, or when there is a head wind or a tail wind.

8. If you depart on a course heading of 125°, what course heading should you follow to return home on this same flight path? Draw a diagram to explain your reasoning.
   125° + 180° = 305°.
   Diagrams will vary.

9. If you depart on a course heading of 200°, what course heading should you follow to return home on the same flight path? Explain your reasoning.
   200° – 180° = 020°. A compass direction greater than 180° must have a return flight direction that is less than 180°. Directions are always 000°–360°.

10. Locate three other airports on your state map. Chart a 030° course line from each airport and extend them for 150 miles.

    a. How are the three course lines related?
       They appear to be parallel.

    b. Where will the course lines intersect?
       They will remain parallel within the continental United States. Above the Arctic Circle, they will converge toward the North Pole.

Plane Tracks

5. If an airplane is flying at a certain rate on a 090° heading while the wind is blowing toward 000° at the same rate, what course is the plane actually tracking?

A 045° course. Because the two forces are equal and perpendicular to each other, the path lies halfway between their directions.

6. A plane is flying at a certain rate on a 090° heading while the wind is blowing it toward 000° at a different rate. What effect will the wind have on the plane's course if:

a. the force of the wind is greater than the airspeed?

If the force of the wind is greater than the airspeed, the path of the plane will follow a track that is less than 045°, approaching 000° as the wind speed increases.

b. the force of the wind is less than the airspeed?

If the force of the wind is less than the airspeed, the path of the plane will follow a course line that is greater than 045°, approaching the desired course of 090° as the wind speed decreases.

Catch My Drift?

1. Why do you think the number of degrees a pilot is off course is referred to as the drift angle?

   Responses will vary.

2. A plane intending to fly on a true course of 090° is actually flying on a ground track of 030°.

   a. Starting near the bottom, left-hand corner of your grid paper, use a circular protractor to chart and label a 090° course line that is 8 inches long.

   b. From the starting point on your grid paper, chart and label a ground track of 030° and extend it for 8 inches.

   c. According to your chart, the drift angle is ___60___ degrees.

3. As the plane continues on a 030° ground track, will it always be the same distance from the intended 090° course line? Explain your reasoning.

   No. The distance off course increases as the distance flown increases.

4. Let 1 inch equal 25 miles. Chart and measure the appropriate lengths on the true course and the ground track to determine the approximate distances off course this plane will be after flying 25, 50, 100, and 200 miles. Record your results in the table.

60° Drift Angle

Miles Traveled	Miles Off Course
25	25
50	50
100	100
200	200

Degrees of Drift

1. Another plane intending to fly on a true course of 090° is actually flying on a 060° ground track.

   a. What is its drift angle? *30°*

   b. Predict the approximate drift for this plane after 100 miles. Explain your reasoning. *Answers will vary.*

   c. On a sheet of grid paper, chart the true course and the ground track from the same point and extend them for 8 inches. Measure the appropriate lengths on the true course and the ground track to determine the approximate distances off course this plane will be after flying 25, 50, 100, and 200 miles. Record your results in the table, and compare them to your predictions.

30° Drift Angle

Miles Traveled	Miles Off Course
25	13
50	26
100	52
200	103

Note: These results should be considered approximate due to the imprecision of measurement, as should the results in 2, 3, and 4.

   d. As the distance this plane travels doubles, the miles off course __doubles__. Explain your reasoning.
     For every 25 miles flown, this plane seems to be about 13 miles off course.

   e. Predict the approximate distance this plane will drift off course after 400 miles and after 1,000 miles. Explain your reasoning. *200 miles, 500 miles. Answers will vary. Some may include the idea. "Since the drift angle is now cut in half, the distance off course seems to be half the distance flown."*

Catch My Drift?

5. Predict the approximate distance off course the plane will be after flying 400 miles and after flying 1,000 miles. Explain your reasoning.
   400 miles, 1,000 miles
   Equal lengths have been marked off on each ray to form a series of isosceles triangles. Since the apex angle is 60°, the equivalent base angles are each $\frac{(180°-60°)}{2}$. This defines an equilateral triangle. Therefore, the distance off course equals the distance flown.

6. As the distance this plane travels doubles, the miles off course __doubles__. Explain your reasoning. *Answers will vary.*

Windy Conditions

1. A pilot is flying at a rate of 100 mph on a true course of 090°. Using a scale of 0.5 inches or 1.5 centimeters equals 10 miles, draw an arrow on the grid paper that shows the true course for the first hour.

2. The wind is blowing due north at the same rate. Using the same scale, draw an arrow showing the effects of the wind for the first hour.

3. Draw a line with an arrow that shows the actual flight path of the plane during the first hour. This is called the *ground track*.
   The grid paper should contain a 10-unit true-course vector at 090°, and 10-unit wind vector at 360° and the resultant ground-track vector.

4. Complete the parallelogram that has the true course and the wind as sides.

   a. What is the relationship of the ground track to this parallelogram?
      The ground track is the diagonal of the parallelogram.

   b. Decide if this plane is flying faster or slower than its airspeed of 100 mph. Explain your reasoning.
      It is flying faster. The length of the flight path after one hour of flying is longer than the length of the true course after one hour of flying.

   c. The ground speed is defined as the plane's speed with respect to the ground. Determine the ground speed. Describe your process.
      The ground speed is about 140 mph. The length of the ground track after one hour is about 140 mph. Since 1 unit = 10 mph, 14 units = 140 mph.

   d. Discuss with your group why this is called a wind parallelogram. *Responses will vary. Some students may include information that defines a parallelogram as a polygon with opposite sides equal and parallel.*

Degrees of Drift

2. A plane is 20° off course. Predict the approximate drift after 1,000 miles. Demonstrate your reasoning. Test your hypothesis.
   ~333 miles
   Since 20° is a third of 60°, it is reasonable to suggest that the drift may also be about a third of the distance flown.

3. After traveling 100 miles, an airplane is 20 miles off course.

   a. How many miles will this plane have flown when it is 80 miles off course?
      Since 80 = 20 × 4, then in 100 × 4 = 400 miles, the plane will be 80 miles off course.

   b. How many miles had it flown when it was 5 miles off course?
      100 miles = 20 miles off course   *using ratios:* $\frac{100}{20} = \frac{x}{2}$
      25 miles = 5 miles off course $x = 25$ *miles*

   c. Determine a possible drift angle for this flight and demonstrate your process.
      Answers will vary. One possible response is given.
      Angle will be less than 20°; $\frac{20}{100} = \frac{1}{5}$ *and* $\frac{1}{5}$ *of* 60° = 12° *off.*

4. What drift angles might a pilot consider insignificant? Explain your reasoning.
   It depends on the distance traveled. Consider a plane off course with a 1° drift angle. After 1,000 miles, it is about 19 miles off course. After 1,000,000 miles, it is about 19,000 miles off course! Using a scale of 1" = 100 miles, a student might draw a 10", 090° course line to represent 1,000 miles. She might then draw a 10", 091° course line to represent 1,000 miles at a 1° drift angle. The distance between the endpoints of the two course lines measures about $\frac{3}{16}$". *Therefore, the drift after 1,000 miles is about 19 miles. If the scale were 1" ≡ 100,000 miles, then the drift after 1,000,000 miles would be about 19,000 miles.*
   It depends on the distance traveled. Consider an airplane with a 001° drift angle. After 1,000 miles, it is 17.4 miles off course. After 1,000,000 miles, it is 17,400 miles off course.

Wind Shifts

1. With your partner, arrange your wind parallelogram to simulate an airplane flying 130 mph on a true course of 180° with a 40-mph wind blowing due east. Trace a copy of your wind parallelogram onto grid paper. Carefully align the endpoints of your parallelogram with the crosshatches on the grid paper, and mark the centers of several holes per side. Connect them with a ruler to complete the outline of the parallelogram. Label the true course, airspeed, wind speed, and wind direction. Indicate and label the ground track.

2. Use your drawing to determine the distance this plane has flown after an hour, its ground speed, the drift angle, and the ground-track direction. Record your data in the table below.
Answers vary due to the imprecision in measurement.

After One Hour	Cardinal Wind Directions			
	East	West	North	South
Distance Flown	136 miles	136 miles	90 miles	170 miles
Ground Speed	136 mph	136 mph	90 mph	170 mph
Drift Angle	17°	17°	0°	0°
Ground Track	163°	197°	180°	180°

3. Discuss with your group how changes in wind direction will affect the plane's ground track, ground speed, and drift angle. Write your predictions here.
Responses will vary. Students may notice that as the wind moves from 090° toward a tail wind at 180°, the length of the diagonal will increase. This represents a ground speed range of 136 mph to 170 mph. The drift angle decreases from 17° to 0°. As the wind shifts from 090° toward a head wind at 000°, the length of the diagonal will decrease. This represents a ground speed decrease from 136 mph to 90 mph. Again, the drift angle will range from 17° to 0°. A drift angle is at its maximum when the plane is flying on a true course that is at a 090° angle to the wind.

Wind Parallelograms

2. As a group, investigate the possibilities of this wind parallelogram.

a. How many different parallelograms can you make with your wind parallelogram? Explain your reasoning.
An infinite number of parallelograms can be made by shifting the sides to alter the angle measures.

b. How do the parallelograms differ?
Angle measurements and diagonal length differ on each parallelogram.

c. How are they similar?
The side lengths remain constant.

3. Where is the ground track located on each wind parallelogram?
It is located along the diagonal.

a. When does the ground track indicate the plane is flying faster than its airspeed?
When the diagonal is longer than the true course, the plane is flying faster than its airspeed.

b. When does the ground track indicate the plane is flying slower than its airspeed?
When the diagonal is shorter than the true course, the plane is flying slower than its airspeed.

c. When does the ground track indicate the plane is flying at the same rate as its airspeed?
Under two conditions: 1. In still air and 2. when the diagonal of the wind parallelogram is equal in length to the true course, the plane's ground track is the same rate as its airspeed. In almost every wind there is, the ground speed will differ from the airspeed.

COMPLETED STUDENT SHEET 3.3 (cont'd)

Wind Shifts

4. Shift your wind parallelogram to demonstrate a situation in which an airplane is flying 130 mph on a true course of 180° with a 40-mph wind blowing in a different cardinal direction, north, south, west, but not east. Trace a copy of this wind parallelogram onto grid paper, again being careful to align the endpoints of your parallelogram with the crosshatches on the grid paper. Label the true course, airspeed, wind speed, and wind direction, then indicate the ground track of the plane. Use your drawing to determine the distance this plane has flown after one hour, its ground speed, ground track, and the drift angle. Record your data in the table above, and compare them to your initial hypotheses.
See answer in question 2. Responses may vary due to the imprecision in measurement.

5. Shift your wind parallelogram to demonstrate another situation, one in which an airplane is flying 130 mph on a true course of 180° with a 40-mph wind blowing in yet another direction. Trace a copy of this wind parallelogram onto grid paper. Label the true course, airspeed, wind speed, and wind direction, and indicate the actual flight path of the plane. Use your drawing to determine the distance this plane has flown after one hour, its ground speed, ground track, and the drift angle. Record your data in the table above, and compare them to your initial hypotheses.
See answer in question 2. Responses may vary due to the imprecision in measurement.

6. As the direction the wind is blowing approaches 180°, the wind becomes a ___tail wind___, and the ground speed is _170 mph_. Discuss with your group and illustrate how the wind parallelogram might show this.
Pictures will vary.

COMPLETED STUDENT SHEET 3.3 (cont'd)

Wind Shifts

7. As the direction the wind is blowing approaches 000°, the wind becomes a ___head wind___, and the ground speed is _90 mph_. Discuss with your group, and illustrate how the wind parallelogram might show this.
Pictures will vary.

8. Based on your data, discuss how wind direction affects the flight path.
Answers will vary but may include the potential flight paths are defined by the various diagonals that follow a circular pattern as the wind moves from a head wind toward a tail wind.

Where the Wind Blows

Wind direction is always reported as the direction from which the wind is blowing. A pilot immediately translates this information into the direction toward which the wind is blowing, which is the direction the wind is blowing the plane.

1. The wind forecast is for a 160° wind. This means the wind is blowing from 160° and is therefore blowing the plane toward 340°. Draw a picture to illustrate this situation, and explain it in words.
   Responses will vary.

2. For each situation below, the wind is blowing from the given direction. Determine toward what direction the wind is blowing the plane.

Wind Direction			
From	Toward	From	Toward
120	300°	210°	030°
040°	220°	255°	075°
090°	270°	290°	110°
060°	240°	330°	150°

3. If you know the direction from which the wind is blowing, how can you calculate the direction toward which it is blowing the plane? Explain your reasoning.
   Add or subtract 180° such that the direction is between 000° and 360°.

Wind Speeds

6. Modify your wind parallelogram of the same flight to represent a 80 mph wind blowing due north, and indicate the ground track of the plane. Use your drawing to determine the distance this plane has flown after one hour, its ground speed, and the drift angle. Record your data in the table, and compare the data to your initial hypotheses.

After One Hour	0 mph	Wind Speeds			
		20 mph	40 mph	80 mph	60 mph
Distance Flown	130 miles	~132 miles	~136 miles	~153 miles	~143 miles
Ground Speed	130 mph	~132 mph	~136 mph	~153 mph	~143 mph
Drift Angle	0°	~9°	~17°	~32°	~25°

7. Discuss with your group what you think the ground speed and drift angle might be for a 60-mph wind. Test your hypothesis.
   Responses will vary.

8. Based on your data, what observations can you make about how wind speed affects the ground speed and the drift angle?
   As wind speed increases, ground speed also increases, but not at a constant rate. As the wind speed increases from 20 mph by 20-mph increments, there is still an initial 2-mph increase, followed by a 4 mph increase, and then a 7-mph increase. The drift angle appears to be increasing at approximately 8°–9° per 20-mph increase in wind speed.

Parallelogram Plots

3. Research the term *vector* and discuss with your group why the true-course and wind arrows are called vectors. Write your hypothesis below and be prepared to explain it to the class.

A vector is a quantity represented by an arrow that indicates both direction and speed. The true-course arrow is a vector because it shows a 090° direction and its length represents flying 130 miles in one hour (the speed). The wind arrow is also a vector because it shows the direction the wind is blowing (000°) and its speed (40 mph).

4. Is the ground track a vector? Explain your reasoning.
Yes. The diagonal of the parallelogram, the ground track, indicates the direction the plane will be flying and the distance the plane will have flown along this path after one hour (representing its speed).

Parallelogram Plots

1. Use tractor strips or Polystrips™ to construct a wind parallelogram that represents an airplane flying 130 mph on a true course of 090° with a 40-mph wind blowing from 180°. Which direction is the wind blowing the plane? Explain your reasoning.
The wind is blowing north toward 000° or 360°.

2. Use a full sheet of grid paper to prepare a set of coordinate axes that indicate the directions north, south, west, and east. Let one unit on the wind parallelogram equal 10 miles.

a. Trace a copy of your wind parallelogram onto the paper, carefully aligning the starting point with the (0, 0) coordinate. Label the true-course and wind arrows.

b. Determine and label the coordinates of the terminal point (endpoint) of the true-course arrow.
Counting a unit as 2 squares on 0.25-inch grid paper or 3 squares on 1.5 cm grid paper, the terminal coordinates are (13, 0).

c. Determine and label the coordinates of the terminal point (endpoint) of the wind arrow. *The coordinates are (0, 4).*

d. List several things you know about the ground track of this flight. *Responses will vary. Students may include that it*
- *is the diagonal of the parallelogram*
- *measures 13.6 units, 6.8 inches or 20.3 cm*
- *represents 136 mph*
- *has terminal coordinates (13, 4).*
- *has a ground track north of the true course with direction ~072°.*

Sum Vectors

1. For each situation below, prepare a separate set of coordinate axes on grid paper with direction arrows indicating north, south, west, and east.

   a. Use the given terminal coordinates to draw the true-course and the wind vector that originate at (0, 0). Label the vectors and coordinates.

   b. Complete the resulting wind parallelogram.

   c. Draw the ground-track vector and determine its terminal coordinates.

Situation	True-Course Vector	Terminal Coordinates Wind Vector	Ground-Track Vector
i	(12, 4)	(2, 3)	(14, 7)
ii	(11, 2)	(⁻5, 3)	(6, 5)
iii	(9, ⁻8)	(⁻1, 4)	(8, ⁻4)
iv	(⁻6, ⁻13)	(⁻2, 4)	(⁻8, ⁻9)

2. Describe how the coordinates of the ground-track vector are related to the coordinates of the wind vector and the true-course vector.
   The x-coordinate of the ground-track vector is the result of adding the x-coordinates of the true-course and the wind vectors. The y-coordinate is the result of adding the true-course and wind vectors' y-coordinates together.

3. The coordinates for the terminal point of a ground-track vector with its initial point at (0, 0) are (12, 7). Plot this and determine the coordinates for the terminal points of the true course and the wind with this ground track. Explain your reasoning.
   There are an infinite number of true-course and wind vector combinations that result in a ground track of (12, 7). Examples: true course (5, 8) and wind (7, ⁻1) and true course (⁻6, 11) and wind (18, ⁻4).

Vector Ventures

1. Prepare a set of coordinate axes on grid paper with direction arrows indicating north, south, west, and east. Let one unit on the grid paper equal 10 miles.

   a. For our purposes, we are going to assume all vectors originate at (0, 0).

   b. On your graph, draw the true-course vector that has terminal coordinates (14, 3). Label both the vector and its coordinates.

   c. Draw the wind vector that has terminal coordinates (2, 4). Again, label both the vector and its coordinates.

   d. Complete the resulting wind parallelogram.

   e. Draw the ground-track vector, determine its terminal coordinates, and label both the vector and its coordinates.
   The ground-track vector's terminal coordinates are (16, 7).

2. Describe your process for completing the wind parallelogram.
   Responses will vary.
   These numbers must be considered approximate due to the imprecision in drawing the course lines.

3. Determine the components of the true-course vector. Explain your reasoning.
   Direction: ~078°   Airspeed: ~144 mph
   Approximate due to the imprecision in drawing.

4. Determine the components of the wind vector. Explain your reasoning.
   Direction: ~026°   Wind speed: ~45 mph
   Approximate due to the imprecision in drawing.

5. Determine the components of the ground-track vector. Explain your calculations.
   Direction: ~067°   Ground speed: ~177 mph
   Approximate due to the imprecision in drawing.

6. What does the ground-track vector represent in your drawings? Explain your reasoning.
   It represents the path and speed of the plane due to the force of the wind as well as the force of the engine.

May the Force Be with You

d. The ground speed of the plane is __90 mph__. Explain your process.
The length of the ground track is 9 units long, which represents approximately 90 mph.

e. After one hour, this plane is ___50___ miles off course.

f. After two hours, this plane is ___100___ miles off course.

g. Would a pilot fly in this wind? Explain your reasoning.
No. The wind would be so strong, the plane would travel less than 100 mph, and the minimum speed for a Cessna 172 is about 126 mph.

May the Force Be with You

Set up the following flight situations on grid paper and use vectors to determine the location of the plane. Let one unit on the grid paper equal 10 miles.

1. A pilot is flying on a true course of 040° at a speed of 130 mph. A wind is blowing from 160° at a speed of 30 mph.

   a. This airplane is tracking on a course of ___030°___.

   b. The drift angle is ___10°___.

   c. Is the wind increasing or decreasing the ground speed of the plane? Explain your reasoning.
   Increasing. The ground-track vector is longer than the true-course vector.

   d. The ground speed of the plane is __147 mph__. Explain your process.
   The length of the ground-track vector is 14.7 units long. This is equivalent to 147 mph.

   e. After one hour, this plane is ___30___ miles off course.

   f. After two hours, this plane is ___60___ miles off course. Explain and illustrate your reasoning.
   The wind is blowing the plane 30 miles off course every hour. Extend the true course and ground track to indicate the distance flown after two hours of flying time, then measure the distance between the vectors.

2. Another pilot is departing from a different airport on a 040° course at a speed of 130 mph. Now the wind is blowing from 010° with a speed of 50 mph.

   a. This airplane is tracking on a course of ___057°___.

   b. The drift angle is ___17°___.

   c. Is the wind increasing or decreasing the ground speed of the plane? Explain your reasoning.
   Decreasing. The ground-track vector is shorter than the true-course vector.

True Heading

Using a wind parallelogram, a pilot determines the true heading, which is the direction the pilot must fly to maintain the plane's desired course.

1. When is the true heading for a flight the same direction as the true course? Explain your reasoning and discuss it with your group.
In still air, during a head wind, and during a tail wind, the true heading is in the same direction as the true course.

2. When is the true heading for a flight a different direction than the true course? Explain your reasoning and discuss it with your group.
When the plane is flying in any wind besides a head wind or tail wind, the true heading is in a different direction than the true course.

3. If an airplane is following a ground track that is north of the true course, what direction will the pilot head the plane in order to arrive at the intended destination? Explain your reasoning.
The pilot will turn the plane south and head into the wind.

4. With your partner, build a wind parallelogram representing an airplane flying at an airspeed of 130 mph with a 40-mph wind.

5. Refer to your drawing from question 1 on Student Sheet 3.3. It represents a true course of 180° with the wind blowing 090° due east. Follow these steps to determine the true heading for this flight.

   a. Align your wind parallelogram with your original grid paper drawing.

   b. One person holds the wind vector strip in place while the other person shifts the parallelogram until the ground-track vector coincides with the true-course vector (or an extension of it) in your drawing.

   c. Accurately outline the second wind parallelogram onto your initial drawing.

True Heading

6. Where is the ground track located for the second wind parallelogram? Explain your reasoning and discuss it with your group. Label it the adjusted ground track (AGT) in your drawing.
It is the diagonal of the second wind parallelogram and it coincides with the true course.

7. Determine the true heading that allows the pilot to fly along the intended true course. Explain your process.
~198°
Explanations will vary.

8. Determine the wind correction angle for this flight. Explain your procedures.
18°
This is the angle measure between the true course and the true heading.

9. When the pilot is flying the true heading, is the plane traveling slower or faster than its airspeed? Explain your reasoning.
Slower. The length of the AGT is less than the length of the true-course vector.

10. Determine the plane's adjusted ground speed. Explain your process.
~124 mph
The AGT is approximately 6.2 inches long for the tractor strips, 18.5 cm, for the Polystrips™, which is equivalent to about 124 mph. Remember these numbers are approximate due to the imprecision of measurement.

Wind Correction

The true heading allows the adjusted ground track to coincide with the true course.

1. With your partner, rebuild a wind parallelogram representing an airplane flying at an airspeed of 130 mph with a 40-mph wind.

2. Refer to your drawings from question 4 on Student Sheet 3.3. Repeat steps 5 a–c given on Student Sheet 5.1 to determine the true heading for a plane flying 130 mph on an intended 180° course. Clearly label your wind parallelograms, and record the data in the table given below.

3. Refer to your drawings from question 5 on Student Sheet 3.3. Repeat steps 5 a–c given on Student Sheet 5.1 to determine the true heading for a plane flying 130 mph on an intended 180° course. Clearly label your wind parallelograms, and record the data in the table given below.

Question	True Course	Wind Direction	Diff Angle	True Heading	Correction Angle	Adjusted Ground Speed
2.						
3.						

Responses will vary.

4. Why does the wind parallelogram method work for determining the true heading?

There are several valid responses. The lengths of the sides remain constant. By shifting them, all possible flight paths based on the wind direction are represented by the various diagonals. Finding the true heading is simply a matter of locating the correct diagonal to coincide with the true course.

Wind Correction

5. Is the adjusted ground-track vector equal to the true-course vector? Explain your reasoning.
   No. They coincide, but they are not necessarily equal in length.

6. Determine the wind-correction angle for each of your flights and record them in the above table.

7. When the pilot in question 2 is flying the true heading, is the plane traveling faster or slower than its airspeed? Explain your reasoning.
   Responses will vary based on the situation.

8. When the pilot in question 3 is flying the true heading, is the plane traveling faster or slower than its airspeed? Explain your reasoning.
   Responses will vary based on the situation.

9. Determine the adjusted ground speed for each of your flight situations and record the results in the above table.
   Responses will vary based on the situation. Remember, these results are approximate.

10. Another pilot flying 130 mph is in a 40-mph wind from 025° and on a true heading of 110°. Determine the true course for this flight. Explain your procedures.
    ~092° Remember, these are approximate.
    One method is to build the wind parallelogram and align it with the wind and true heading. This provides the diagonal representing the true-course direction.

Diagonals and Differences

1. With your partner, follow these steps to construct a second wind parallelogram that will give the coordinates for the true heading and the adjusted ground track for each vector display from Student Sheet 4.4.

   a. Open the compass span to the length of the true-course vector. Place the compass point on the terminal point of the wind vector and draw an arc that intersects the true-course vector or an extension of it.

   b. Determine and label the coordinates for this point of intersection that represents the terminal point for the adjusted ground track (AGT). Connect this point to the terminal point of the wind vector, creating a new vector. This new vector and the wind vector can then be used to create a second wind parallelogram that has as its diagonal the AGT vector.

   c. Complete the second wind parallelogram and outline it with a highlighter.

   d. Determine and label the coordinates of the terminal point for the true-heading vector. Record the data in the table.

		Terminal Coordinates		
Situation	Course Vector	Wind Vector	Adjusted Ground Track	True Heading
i	(12, 4)	(2, 3)	(14.5, 4.8)	(12.5, 1.8)
ii	(11, 2)	(⁻5, 3)	(6, 1)	(11, ⁻2)
iii	(9, ⁻8)	(⁻1, 4)	(6.25, ⁻5.5)	(7.25, ⁻9.5)
iv	(⁻6, ⁻13)	(⁻2, 4)	(⁻4.5, ⁻10)	(⁻2.5, ⁻14)

Diagonals and Differences

2. Describe your process for completing the second wind parallelogram. *Responses will vary.*

3. In each situation, is the plane flying slower or faster than its airspeed? Explain your reasoning.
   i. *Faster. The AGT vector is longer than the true-course vector.*
   ii. *Slower. The AGT vector is shorter than the true-course vector.*
   iii. *Slower.*
   iv. *Slower.*

4. Describe how the coordinates of the true heading are related to the other coordinates.
   Once you know the coordinates for the AGT, the true-heading coordinates can be determined by subtracting corresponding coordinates of the wind vector from the AGT vector.

What Makes an Airplane Fly?

1. Cut a 2-inch strip of notebook paper. Place one end of it against your lower lip. Gently blow along the upper surface of the strip. Describe what happens. *The strip rises.*

2. Try the above experiment after you have fastened a paper clip on the end of the strip. How many paper clips can you lift in this way? *Responses will vary.*

3. Remove the paper clips. Hold the strip of paper in your hand and run around the room. What do you observe? *The strip rises.*

4. Based on the paper's behavior, does it matter whether you move the air over the paper or move the paper through the air? Explain your reasoning. *No. Either way, the strip rises.*

5. What do you think will happen to two sheets of notebook paper if you hold them about 4 inches apart and blow between them? *Responses will vary.*

6. Try the above experiment and describe what actually happens. Did the results surprise you? Explain why you think this occurs. *The two strips of paper come together because the air pressure on the outside of each strip is greater than the pressure between the strips.*

Track and True

1. Plot the following navigational situations on grid paper. Determine the wind parallelogram for each problem. Locate the second wind parallelogram to determine the true heading in order to maintain the desired course. Then calculate the adjusted ground speed (AGS). Record the information in the table provided. Let one unit equal 10 miles.

a. Situation A: A plane is flying on a true course of 080° at a speed of 165 mph. The wind is blowing from 130° at a speed of 40 mph.

True Course	Airspeed	Wind From	Wind Toward	Wind Speed	Correction Angle	True Heading	AGS
080°	165 mph	130°	310°	40 mph	012°	091°	~135 mph

b. Situation B: Another plane is departing on a true course of 230° at a speed of 140 mph. The wind is blowing from 350° at a speed of 35 mph.

True Course	Airspeed	Wind From	Wind Toward	Wind Speed	Correction Angle	True Heading	AGS
230°	140 mph	350°	170°	35 mph	012°	242°	~155 mph

2. Refer to question 1 on Student Sheet 4.6. Complete the flight plan by determining the true heading the pilot will fly in order to arrive at the intended destination. Determine the adjusted ground speed as well. Record the information below. *Responses will vary based on situation.*

True Course	Airspeed	Wind From	Wind Toward	Wind Speed	Correction Angle	True Heading	AGS	Distance

3. Based on the adjusted ground speed above, calculate the revised flight time for your journey. *Responses will vary based on situation.*

GRID PAPER 0.25 INCH

GRID PAPER 0.5 CENTIMETER